The Vikings

**Recent Titles in
Historical Facts and Fictions**

The Victorian World: Facts and Fictions
Ginger S. Frost

The Vikings

Facts and Fictions

Kirsten Wolf and
Tristan Mueller-Vollmer

Historical Facts and Fictions

BLOOMSBURY ACADEMIC
NEW YORK • LONDON • OXFORD • NEW DELHI • SYDNEY

BLOOMSBURY ACADEMIC
Bloomsbury Publishing Inc
1385 Broadway, New York, NY 10018, USA
50 Bedford Square, London, WC1B 3DP, UK
29 Earlsfort Terrace, Dublin 2, Ireland

BLOOMSBURY, BLOOMSBURY ACADEMIC and the Diana logo
are trademarks of Bloomsbury Publishing Plc

First published in the United States of America by ABC-CLIO 2018
Paperback edition published by Bloomsbury Academic 2024

Copyright © Bloomsbury Publishing Inc, 2024

Cover photo: Viking man and longship. (Corey A. Ford/Dreamstime.com)

All rights reserved. No part of this publication may be reproduced or
transmitted in any form or by any means, electronic or mechanical,
including photocopying, recording, or any information storage or retrieval
system, without prior permission in writing from the publishers.

Bloomsbury Publishing Inc does not have any control over, or responsibility for,
any third-party websites referred to or in this book. All internet addresses given
in this book were correct at the time of going to press. The author and publisher
regret any inconvenience caused if addresses have changed or sites have
ceased to exist, but can accept no responsibility for any such changes.

Library of Congress Cataloging-in-Publication Data
Names: Wolf, Kirsten, 1959- | Mueller-Vollmer, Tristan, author.
Title: The Vikings : facts and fictions / Kirsten Wolf and Tristan
Mueller-Vollmer.
Description: Santa Barbara, CA: ABC-CLIO, LLC, [2018] |
Series: Historical facts and fictions | Includes bibliographical references and index.
Identifiers: LCCN 2018012769 (print) | LCCN 2018022870 (ebook) |
ISBN 9781440862991 (eBook) | ISBN 9781440862984 (hardcopy: alk. paper)
Subjects: LCSH: Vikings. | Civilization, Viking.
Classification: LCC DL65 (ebook) |
LCC DL65.W6552 2018 (print) | DDC 948/.022–dc23
LC record available at https://lccn.loc.gov/2018012769

ISBN: HB: 978-1-4408-6298-4
PB: 979-8-7651-2014-9
ePDF: 978-1-4408-6299-1
eBook: 979-8-2161-6201-8

Series: Historical Facts and Fictions

To find out more about our authors and books visit www.bloomsbury.com
and sign up for our newsletters.

Contents

Preface	vii
Introduction	ix
1. Vikings Were One Nation	1
2. All Scandinavians Were Vikings	25
3. Vikings Were Barbarians	37
4. All Vikings Were Pagan	53
5. Vikings Were Hated by Their Peers	69
6. Wives of Vikings Had Equal Rights	91
7. Vikings Had Primitive Weapons	109
8. Vikings Were Unhygienic	123
9. Vikings Wore Horned Helmets	133
10. Vikings Carved the Blood Eagle	145
11. Vikings Drank Out of Skull Cups	155
Bibliography	175
Index	177

Preface

The allure of the Vikings never ends. They have been a source of immense fascination for centuries. Historians, archaeologists, and literary historians have devoted innumerable books and articles to narratives, discussions, and examinations of their endeavors. Some scholars have focused on the more negative side of the activities of the Vikings, which is, of course, the raids and—by extension—the harm these northern pirates caused many innocent civilians in the British Isles, Germany, the Netherlands, France, and elsewhere. Other scholars have concentrated on the more positive aspects of the activities of the Vikings. Among other things, they have emphasized the Vikings' exceptional seafaring skills, which enabled them to crisscross half of the world—known and unknown at the time—in their longships; their expertise in engineering, which resulted in such masterpieces as the geometrically planned Danish fortresses and the rampart Danevirke (Defense of the Danes); and their sensitive noses for political weaknesses in countries outside of Scandinavia, which told them when it would be opportune for them to strike.

Given the fascination with the Vikings and the inordinate attention they have received not only by scholars but also amateur enthusiasts, it is not surprising that over the centuries, some unfortunate misconceptions about the Vikings have arisen. Despite efforts by scholars to make corrections and set things straight, some of these misconceptions continue to be perpetuated, especially in popular culture, such as movies and computer games—presumably because they help what makes a good story about the Vikings an even better story.

In this book, we attempt to address these misconceptions. Most readers probably know that the Vikings did not wear horned helmets, did not drink out of skull cups, and did not carve the blood eagle. These are all Viking clichés. Some readers may also know that that not all Scandinavians were Vikings and that many Scandinavians worked as, for example, peaceful farmers, blacksmiths, carpenters, traders, and fishermen without ever setting foot on a ship and engaging in a raid. Similarly, some readers may know that the Vikings were not as primitive as they have sometimes been portrayed. Other readers may be surprised to learn in this book not only that some of the Vikings were Christian but also that some of the Vikings ended up serving in the interest of the rulers of the regions in which they pillaged.

Each of the eleven chapters in this volume is prefaced by a short introduction explaining the origin of the misconception about what happened. This is followed by two sections. One describes how the erroneous idea or misconception became popular. The other describes how and when the misconception was corrected. Both sections are accompanied by one or two primary source documents.

We are grateful to George Butler, who invited us to write this book. His help and guidance throughout the process of compiling this book are much appreciated.

Introduction

The term *Viking Age* is a late construction by modern historians, archaeologists, literary historians, novelists, and artists. Obviously, the Vikings themselves did not know that they were living in the Viking Age.

In textbooks, the beginning of the Viking Age is typically associated with the plundering and destruction of the church and monastery of Lindisfarne, just off the Northumbrian coast, in 793. In the three centuries that followed, the Vikings changed the political world of northern and western Europe in no small way. The Danish Vikings especially seem to have focused on the British Isles, Germany, the Netherlands, and France, where they became known as a dreaded military force. Although the Norwegian Vikings also participated in raids, they appear to have concentrated mainly on the colonization of the islands in the North Atlantic: the Shetland Islands, Orkney Islands, Faroe Islands, and Iceland. The Swedish Vikings were not particularly innocent either, but typically they went eastward as traders, where they thrust up the rivers of Russia to the Caspian and Black Seas and established themselves as Rus along the way. As for the end of the Viking Age, it is commonly associated with the famous battle at Stamford Bridge near York, England, in 1066, when the Normans (descendants of the Vikings) crossed the channel to invade England. Since, however, the Scandinavians, who by then were well established in the British Isles, did not disappear right away, it seems practical to regard the late 11th century as marking the end of the Viking Age. Broadly speaking, therefore, the Viking Age spans the period 800–1100.

The image of the Vikings has undergone transformations over the years. Most of the earliest sources were written by Christians, who documented the sufferings of their fellow citizens either based on eyewitness accounts or on the basis of stories they had heard about their raids and styles of life. These sources include works such as the *Anglo-Saxon Chronicle*, *Cogadh Gaedhel re Gallaibh* (*The War between the Irish and the Foreigners*), *The Annals of St-Bertin*, and Adam of Bremen's *Gesta Hammaburgensis ecclesiae potificum* (*Activities of the Prelates of the Church of Hamburg*). Muslims, too, wrote about the Vikings, although most of these are geographical works. An important source in this respect is Ibn Fadlān's account of the Rus near the middle Volga in Russia. Needless to say, the early portrayal of the Vikings is quite negative. If one combines the description of the Vikings in writings of contemporary Christians and Muslims, the Vikings were filthy, testosterone-driven, northern brutes intent on killing, maiming, raping, and plundering. Some of these depictions greatly contributed to what was later considered misconceptions about the Vikings—such as the notion that all Scandinavians came from one area and also that they all were pagan, barbarian, and unhygienic.

Aside from Scandinavian and Icelandic medieval works—notably the Sagas of Icelanders, a group of approximately 40 sagas composed in Iceland during the 13th, 14th, and 15th centuries, about Icelandic farmer-chieftains from the period of settlement (870–930) to the mid-11th century, and the early-13th century *Gesta Danorum* (*Deeds of the Danes*) by the Danish Saxo Grammaticus—in which the Vikings were glorified, it was not until the 18th century that a more romanticized image of the Vikings began to appear. Two Swedish writers were particularly instrumental in propagating this new ideal of the Vikings. One was Erik Gustaf Geijer (1783–1874), a historian, poet, philosopher, and composer. His famous poem *Vikingen* (*The Viking*), which portrayed the Viking as a heroic Norseman, did much to rehabilitate attitudes toward the Vikings. Geijer was also a founding member of *Götiska förbundet* (The Geatish Society). The mission of this men's society, which was founded in 1811 by Swedish poets and authors, was to deliberate Scandinavian antiquity, encourage patriotic spirit, and advance archaeological research in Scandinavia in an attempt to raise the moral tone in Sweden. The society published a magazine entitled *Iduna* (named after the goddess Idun, who provided the gods with life-sustaining apples) in which poetry, translations of Old Norse-Icelandic literary works, and articles on Scandinavian literature and mythology were published. The other was Esaias Tegnér (1782–1847), a professor of Greek language and later bishop of Växsjö. Tegnér, too, was a member of *Götiska förbundet*, and in 1820, he published in *Iduna* a section of his epic *Frithiofs saga*. Two years later, he published five more cantos, and in 1825 the entire poem appeared. The poem became famous throughout Europe and was applauded by such famous writers as Johann Wolfgang von Goethe (1749–1832). The publication of *Frithiofs saga* made Tegnér one of the best-known poets in Europe, and the poem was translated into many languages.

A similar rehabilitation took place in Victorian England. Early editions of Scandinavian and Icelandic works reached the British Isles and caught the attention of literary historians, archaeologists, historians, and linguists, who subsequently began to look into their own past and became fascinated. As pointed out by Andrew Wawn, even the court of Queen Victoria (1819–1901) was affected by this renewed interest in the Vikings:

> There were claims that Victoria was descended from Odinn; that the entire Hanoverian royal family was related to Ragnarr Hairy-Breeches, a mighty Viking chief; and that King Haraldr Bluetooth was an ancestor of the Danish-born Princess of Wales. The Queen's principal physician, Sir Henry Holland, was a trail-blazing Iceland explorer, and under his influence a native Icelandic scholar was received at court, where he recited an eddic-style Icelandic poem. (http://www.bbc.co.uk/history/abcuebt/vikings/revival_01.shtml)

Several other misconceptions about the Vikings may be traced to the 18th and 19th centuries and the enthusiastic scholars and artists during this period. These include the horned helmets, the cups made from the skulls of enemies, and the carving of the blood eagle.

This constructed and romanticized image of the Viking became very powerful and was relished by the Germans, who as early as the mid-19th century promoted the idea of a shared Scandinavian and German heritage. Examples include the German brothers Jacob Grimm (1785–1863) and Wilhelm Grimm (1786–1859), who published songs from the *Poetic Edda*, and Richard Wagner (1813–1883), who composed the *Ring of the Nibelungs* based on Germanic and Nordic mythology. German philosopher and cultural critic Friedrich Nietzsche (1844–1900) was, at least initially, a friend of Wagner and became influenced by him. It is likely that to some extent the development of Nietzsche's concept of the *Übermensch* (superior man), who justified the human race, was inspired by Wagner and his interest in the Germanic past. In time, the Übermensch—a man who could rise above conventional Christian morality to create and impose his own values—became identified with the Aryan race, which, in turn, became identified with tall, fair-skinned, blue-eyed, blond people in northern Europe and, in particular, with the

Scandinavians, the progeny of the Vikings, who were considered particularly pure in terms of ethnic breed. After the defeat of the Germans in World War I, the concept of a pure race became a matter of party politics in Germany, which lasted well into the 1930s, when the Vikings and Norse symbols and mythology were used in an attempt to promote the image of an Aryan master race. Adolf Hitler (1889–1945), who eventually became the leader of the Nazi party, adopted not only this idea of race but also the Darwinian idea of the survival of the fittest. Hitler and his party used warrior images of the Vikings on recruitment posters, and one unfortunate outcome of this was the establishment of a brigade—named Viking—consisting of Norwegian sympathizers, who were sent to attack the Russians toward the end of World War II. It is well known that the war resulted in an ethnic cleansing of unparalleled proportions, and the targets were not only Jews but also the sick and the elderly and the young and the poor. Moreover, in communist Russia, the ideology of Slavic racial purity caused a complete denial of the fact that the Rus had a hand in the foundation of their principalities. Unfortunately, there are still lingering effects of the idea of the pure race. These are the white supremacists, who misappropriate Viking Age symbols with the false idea that the Vikings existed in pure white racial isolation. In Europe, the supremacists dress up in Viking outfit as antirefugee protesters, and in the United States, they band together as hate groups and invoke the god Odin and Vinland, the name given to the area in North America where the first Norseman set foot.

After World War II, the image of the Vikings shifted once again—perhaps because people were tired of warfare and warriors and just wanted peace, but more likely because of new archaeological finds and a somewhat more critical and scholarly attitude toward not only those archaeological finds but also the historical and literary sources. There is now a tendency to focus on the peaceful side of the Vikings and their activities. Among other things, scholars have concentrated on their political acumen and awareness of the state of affairs in the countries west, south, and east of Scandinavia; their extraordinary navigational skills, which enabled them to discover and settle new lands; their expertness as engineers, which resulted in phenomenally planned fortresses and ramparts; their ability to find trade routes and set up trading centers; and their remarkable artistic skills and sense of aesthetics testified to by the many artifacts they left behind. The misconception that the Vikings were protofeminists and multiculturalists may be assigned to this era of Viking apologists and revisionists.

However, not everyone is willing to accept the image of the reformed and rehabilitated Viking. Among other things, an exhibition in the British Museum in 2004 of Viking artifacts became a source of heated debate in British newspapers, with some journalists and scholars denouncing the revisionist or apologist attitude toward the Vikings and insisting that the Vikings were, as first thought by foreign writers, violent and brutal raiders.

The Vikings continue to be a source of fascination. Most likely they will be for a long time, during which their history and the attitudes toward them will be revisited and revised again and again. Despite their swords, spears, axes, shields, and not least their defensive armor, they turned out to prove malleable to the needs of ideological, political, and societal currents for centuries. Would the Vikings approve? No one will ever know.

1

Vikings Were One Nation

What People Think Happened

Some people think that the Vikings were one nation with the same language, culture, religion, dress habits, and so on. The misconception likely has its origin in the times of the Viking raids in Europe, when non-Scandinavian medieval sources describing the events often simply referred to the invaders as *Nordmanni* (Northmen) (Price 2000, 118). English sources, for example, use the term *Danes*, regardless of the Vikings' origin. To the victims of the raiders, it did not matter which regions the attackers belonged to; the writers focused on the traumatic events themselves, noting simply that the attackers were non-Christians, and did not make distinctions between different groups of Vikings. The entry for the year 787 in the *Anglo-Saxon Chronicle* illustrates the point in that it uses the terms *Northmen* and *Danes* interchangeably, despite also mentioning Hordaland (a region in Norway) as their origin: "Here Beorhtric took King Offa's daughter Eadburh. And in his days came first 3 ships of Northmen from Hordaland: and then the reeve rode there and wanted to compel them to go to the king's town because he did not know what they were; and then they killed him. These were the first ships of the Danish men which sought out the land of the English race" (Swanton 2000, 55).

In addition, the language spoken in Scandinavia during the Viking Age and early Middle Ages was generally known as *dǫnsk tunga* (Danish tongue) among Scandinavians, which suggests a common language. The term is used in the 13th-century Icelandic law code *Grágás* (Grey

Goose) and other early sources. In his prologue to *Heimskringla* (*Disc of the World*), Snorri Sturluson (1178/1179–1241) states: "In this book I have written down old accounts about the chieftains who had dominion in the North and were speakers of the Danish tongue" (Snorri Sturluson 1964, 3).

The idea of the Vikings as one distinct, unified culture appears to have gained further ground or maybe even been promoted by later centuries' imaginations of the past, when in Scandinavia the Vikings became a powerful symbol of national identity.

How the Story Became Popular

In the 19th century, Vikings and Old Norse-Icelandic literature became a popular subject of study and obsession in Europe. This interest has its origin in the Romantic Nationalism movement, when Europeans became fascinated with their Germanic past, which in their minds was wild and irrational compared to the classical values of order and rationalism. The Germanic tribes came to be regarded no longer as destructive barbarians but rather as noble savages possessing valuable cultural traits. The Goths—the Germanic tribe known for contributing to the downfall of the Western Roman Empire—became a kind of umbrella term used for the bearers of Germanic culture. The Scottish historian John Pinkerton emphasized the newfound interest in the Goths and Germanic culture in his dissertation: "We, misled by a puerile love of the Romans, revile the ruder Goths, our fathers, as despisers of learning and the arts . . . the Goths were the friends of every elegant art, and useful science" (Pinkerton 1798, I 4). Prior to the 19th century, there had already been interest in the Germanic past in 17th-century Sweden, when the movement known as Gothicism glorified the Swedish tribe of the Geats, who were held to be of the same origin as the Goths. The movement rose and fell, but reemerged in the 19th century. In 1811, *Götiska Förbundet* (The Geatish Society) was founded, which, incidentally, helped spread the image of the horn-helmeted Viking (see chapter 9).

Inspired by this enthusiasm about the ancient Germanic past, the English began to investigate their own identity with their Anglo-Saxon and, by extension, Norse roots. Fascination with the Vikings spread like wildfire, and Viking novels began to appear by the dozen in the mid-19th century, with titles such as *The Viking* (1849), *The Northmen: The Sea-Kings and Vikings* (1852), *The Champion of Odin: Or Viking Life in Days of Old*

(1885), and *Graves of the Northmen* (1893). The terms *Vikings, Norsemen,* and *Northmen* were used liberally and for the most part interchangeably in English, identifying the Viking Age with the general geographic region of Scandinavia. No distinction was made among Danes, Norwegians, and Swedes. In his preface to the novel *The Viking* (1888), Elwyn A. Barron exemplifies the obsession with a generalized and romanticized northern world: "[T]hat region whence sprang so many of the great romances and dramas, the weird and mystical North" (6). Although the Victorians were aware of the geographic and therefore also cultural expanses of the Viking world, they were even more eager to seek the roots of English culture in the early medieval Norse past. The result was that the Vikings became a constructed concept, a mythical, unified culture and ancestor to Western civilization.

Alongside the new interest in Vikings and Norse culture also came darker ideas of northern European racial supremacy. Among those promoting the idea was the French count Joseph Arthur de Gobineau, who in his *Essai sur l'inégalité des races humaines* (*An Essay on the Inequality of the Human Races*, 1853–1855) claimed that the Aryan race, which he identified with *la race germanique* (the Germanic race), was superior to all others in the world. The Norse were perceived as especially pure and uncontaminated; accordingly, they were very appealing to proponents of racial theories. The cultural diversity of the Viking world was ignored, and Vikings became a homogenous race of tall, strong, blond, and blue-eyed Norsemen. Another infamous proponent of the 19th-century racial theories was Richard Wagner. On September 22, 1869, his opera *Das Rheingold* (*The Rhinegold*), the first part in the cycle *Ring des Nibelungen* (*The Ring of the Nibelung*) premiered in Munich, Germany. Wagner based his *Ring* cycle on Germanic mythology but relied heavily on Scandinavian sources. Wagner's operas had a profound impact on the image of Vikings, who became a symbol for all things Germanic. In the late 19th century, Justus Barth, professor of anatomy at the University of Kristiania (now Oslo), Norway, even described Nordic skulls as belonging to *Vikingtypen* (the Viking type) (Hochman 2015, 85). Later in the early to mid-20th century, the Nazis appropriated Norse symbols and mythology as part of their pan-Germanic doctrine, and used them, among other things, to attract Danes and Norwegians to the SS (Tveskov and Erlandson 2007, 35).

The idea of Vikings as one homogenous cultural group has been prominent in popular culture since the proliferation of novels during the Victorian Era. With the advent of moving pictures, silent films about Vikings appeared, such as *The Viking Bride* (1907), *The Viking's Daughter*

(1908), and *The Viking Queen* (1914). The first Technicolor film with a full soundtrack was *The Viking* (1928). It was later followed by the hugely popular *The Vikings* (1958) starring Kirk Douglas, Tony Curtis, and Ernest Borgnine. In these films, the romanticized image of Vikings takes precedence over historical accuracy. The Norse are portrayed as rugged, impulsive, untamed individuals, who appeal to their audience as symbols of defiance and rebellion. At the end of the 20th and beginning of the 21st century, renewed interest in Vikings gave rise to still more films, such as *The 13th Warrior* (1999) and *Valhalla Rising* (2009), and the popular TV series *Vikings*, created by Michael Hirst and starring Travis Fimmel and Katheryn Winnick.

Computer and video games have also done much to promote the idea of Vikings as a unified culture. In styles ranging from classic 1980s two-dimensional side-scrollers and turn-based roleplay to strategic micromanagement and first-person perspective with ultrarealistic graphics, the many games involving Vikings or Norse culture testify to the continued appeal of Vikings and also to the romanticized image of Norsemen that was created during the 19th century. Since the 1980s, dozens of Viking-themed computer and video games for various platforms have been released. Examples include "Valhalla" (1983), "The Saga of Erik the Viking" (1984), "Ragnarok" (1992), "Rune" (2000), "The Elder Scrolls V: Skyrim" (2011), "Viking: Battle for Asgard" (2012), "Völgarr the Viking" (2013), "Jotun: Valhalla Edition" (2015), "Viking Squad" (2015), "For Honor" (2017), "Northgard" (2017), "Vikings: Wolves of Midgard" (2017), and "Expeditions: Vikings" (2017). Even some not explicitly Norse-themed games have perpetuated the idea of a homogenous Viking culture. One example is the medieval-strategy empire-building game "Age of Empires II: The Age of Kings," released by Ensemble Studios and Microsoft for Windows and Mac operating systems in 1999. As the sequel to "Age of Empires I" (set in European antiquity), the game covers roughly the time period 500–1500 CE and features 13 different cultures or civilizations to choose from and advance through the ages. One of the civilizations, which is called simply *Vikings*, features the unique combat units of berserkers and longboats, and the Viking "wonder" (a strategically valuable building requiring a large number of resources to build) has the physical appearance of the stave church in Borgund, Norway. Although there are numerous other historical inaccuracies and vast generalizations in the game, the definition of the Vikings as one cultural group falls within the misconception of a homogenous cultural identity across Scandinavia during the Viking Age.

PRIMARY DOCUMENTS
ESAIAS TEGNÉR, *FRITHIOFS SAGA* (1825)

Esaias Tegnér (1782–1846) was a Swedish professor and author and a member of the Geatish Society. Deeply interested in the Norse past, Tegnér composed an epic poem based on the Old Norse-Icelandic saga, Frithiofs saga, *which was published in its entirety in 1825. The poem was influential throughout Europe. The many references to Norse gods, Valhalla, and a generalized "Northland" contributed to the romanticized image of the Viking, emphasizing a common Norse culture rather than regional differences.*

II. KING BELE AND THORSTEN VIKINGSSON.

KING BELE in his palace stood, on his sword he leaned,
And by him Thorsten Vikingsson, his old, tried friend;
The comrade who for eighty years his wars did share,
Scarred as a monument was he, and white his hair.

So stand two aged temples, midst mountains high,
Both with age tottering, to ruin nigh;
Yet words of wisdom still on the walls we see,
And on the roof pictures of antiquity.

"My day is setting fast," King Bele said;
"Tasteless the mead; I feel the helmet's weight;
Dim are my glazing eyes to mortal state.
But Valhall' dawns more near; I feel my fate.

"So my two sons, with thine, I've called to me;
Together they're united, as have been we;
Once more to warn the young birds am I fain,
Ere from a dead man's tongue all words be vain."

Then to the hall they entered in, as he had willed:
The elder, Helge, whose dark brow with gloom was filled;
His days in temples spent he, with spaemen hoary,
And now from sacrificing came, his hands still gory.

Then came the younger, Halfdan, with flaxen hair;
His countenance was noble, but soft and fair;

As if in sport, a heavy falchion bearing.
Like a young maid a warrior's armor wearing.

And last, in azure mantle, came Frithiof tall.
By a full head in stature outmeasuring them all;
He stood between the brothers as glorious day
Stands between rosy dawning and twilight gray.

"My children," quoth the king, "my day doth wane;
Rule in fraternal peace, in union reign;
For union, like the ring upon the spear.
Makes strong what, wanting it, were worthless gear.

"Let Vigour be your country's sentinel,
And blooming Peace within securely dwell;
To shelter, not to harm, your weapons wield.
And let your subjects' bulwark be your shield.

"An unwise ruler devastates his land;
All monarchs' might in people's strength must stand;
Soon the green splendor of the tree is fled,
If from the naked rock its roots be fed.

"Four pillars to uphold it, Heaven doth own;
Kingdoms are based on one—on Law alone.
Danger is near where might can sway the Ting;
Right guards the land, and glorifies the king.

"Helge! in Disarsal the gods do dwell;
But not, like snails, within a narrow shell;
Far as the day can shine, or echo sound.
Far as the thought can flee, the gods are found.

"Oft err the entrails of the offered hawk;
False, though deep-cut, is many a Runenbalk;
But in the open heart and honest eye
Odin hath written Runes that ne'er can lie.

"Helge! be not severe—be firm alone;
By bending most the truest sword is known;

Mercy adorns a king, as flowers a shield;
More than all winter can one spring-day yield.

"A friendless man, however mighty he,
Fadeth deserted, like a bark-stripped tree;
With roots refreshed, though fierce the storm-winds strive,
By friendship's stream thou may'st securely thrive.

"Boast not thy father's fame—'tis his alone;
A bow thou canst not bend is scarce thine own.
What can a buried glory be to thee?
By its own force the river gains the sea.

"Gladness, O Halfdan, doth the wise adorn;
But folly, most of all in kings, brings scorn!
Mix hops with honey, when thou mead wilt brew;
Make thy sports sterner, and thy weapon too.

"None is too learned, however wise he be.
That many knowledge lack, too well know we;
Despised the witless sitteth at the feast;
The learned hath the ear of every guest.

"To trusty comrade, or to friend in war.
Be thy way near, although his home be far;
Yet let thy foeman's house, where'er it lie,
Be ever distant, though thou pass it by.

"Thy confidence to many shun to give;
Full barns we lock; the empty, open leave;
Choose one in whom to trust—more seek not thou;
The world, O Halfdan, knows what three men know!"

After the king rose Thorsten. Thus spake he:
"Odin alone to seek ill fitteth thee;
We've shared each hap, O king, our whole lives through.
And death, I trust, we'll share together too.

"Full many a warning Time hath whispered me,
Son Frithiof, which I gladly give to thee;

As on the tombstones high perch Odin's birds.
So on the lips of age hang wisdom's words.

"Honor the gods; for every good and harm
Cometh from above, like sunshine and like storm;
Deep into hearts they see, and many mourn
A lifelong sorrow for one short hour's scorn.

"Honor the king! Let one man rule with might;
Day hath but one eye, many hath the night
Let not the better grudge against the best;
The sword must have a hilt to hold it fast.

"High strength is Heaven's gift; yet little prize
It brings its owner, if he be not wise;
A bear with twelve men's strength can one man kill:
As shield 'gainst sword, set law against thy will.

"The proud are feared by few, hated by all;
And insolence, O Frithiof, brings a fall.
Men, mighty once, I've seen on crutches borne,
And fortune changeth like storm-blasted corn.

"Praise not the day before the night arrive;
Mead till 'tis drunk, or counsel till it thrive;
Youth trusteth soon to many an idle word;
Need proves a friend, as battle proves a sword.

"Trust not to one night's ice, to spring-day snow,
To serpent's slumber, or to maiden's vow;
For heart of woman turneth like a wheel.
And 'neath the snowy breast doth falsehood dwell.

"Thyself must perish, all thou hast must fade;
One thing alone on earth is deathless made—
That is, the dead man's glory; therefore thou
Will what is right, and what is noble, do."

So warned the graybeards in the royal hall,
As later warned the Skald in Havamal;

From mouth to mouth went words of wisdom round.
Which, whispered still, through Northland's hills resound.

Then both full many a hearty memory named
Of their true friendship, in the Northland famed;
How, faithful unto death, in joy or need.
Like two clasp'd hands, together they had stayed.

"Sons! back to back our stand we ever made;
So ever to each Norne a shield displayed;
And now, we aged, to Valhalla haste;
Oh! with our sons may their sires' spirits rest!"

Much spake the king of Frithiof's valor good,
His hero-might excelling royal blood;
And Thorsten much of future fame to crown
The Asa sons, who should the Northland own.

"And if ye hold together, ye mighty three.
Your conqueror the Northland ne'er shall see;
For might, by lofty station firmly held.
Is like the steel rim round a golden shield.

"And my dear daughter—tender rose-bud!—greet
In tranquil silence bred, as most is meet;
Defend her; let the storm-wind ne'er have power
To plant upon his crest my late-born flower.

"Helge! on thee I lay a father's care;
Guard, like a daughter dear, my Ingborg fair;
Force breaks a noble soul, but mildness leads
Both man and maid to good and noble deeds.

"Now, children, lay us in two lofty graves
Down by the sea-shore, near the deep blue waves:
Their sounds shall to our souls be music sweet,
Singing our dirge as on the strand they beat

"When round the hills the pale moonlight is thrown,
And midnight dews fall on the Bauta-stone,

We'll sit, O Thorsten, in our rounded graves.
And speak together o'er the gentle waves.

"And now, ye sons beloved, fare ye well;
We go to Allfather, in peace to dwell.
As weary rivers long to reach the sea.
With you may Frey and Thor and Odin be!"

Source: Tegnér, Esaias. 1867. *Frithiof's Saga*, translated by William Lewery Blackley. New York: Leypoldt and Holt. 8–15.

HENRY WADSWORTH LONGFELLOW, *THE SKELETON IN ARMOR* (1841)

Henry Wadsworth Longfellow (1807–82), author of the poem The Skeleton in Armor *(1841), was inspired by a skeleton discovered in Fall River, Massachusetts, in 1832. Theories as to the cultural identity of the skeleton ranged from a Native American and an early European colonizer to a more exotic Phoenician, Carthaginian, or Egyptian person. In this poem, the source of which is clearly the attempted Norse settlement in North America, Wadsworth considers the skeleton to belong to a Norseman. The poem encapsulates the Victorian image of the romanticized Viking and reveals the interest in the Norse as symbols of national identity.*

"SPEAK! speak! thou fearful guest!
Who, with thy hollow breast
Still in rude armor drest,
Comest to daunt me!
Wrapt not in Eastern balms,
But with thy fleshless palms
Stretched, as if asking alms,
Why dost thou haunt me?"

Then, from those cavernous eyes
Pale flashes seemed to rise,
As when the Northern skies
Gleam in December;
And, like the water's flow
Under December's snow,
Came a dull voice of woe
From the heart's chamber.

"I was a Viking old!
My deeds, though manifold,
No Skald in song has told,
No Saga taught thee!
Take heed, that in thy verse
Thou dost the tale rehearse,
Else dread a dead man's curse;
For this I sought thee.

"Far in the Northern Land,
By the wild Baltic's strand,
I, with my childish hand,
Tamed the gerfalcon;
And, with my skates fast-bound,
Skimmed the half-frozen Sound,
That the poor whimpering hound
Trembled to walk on.

"Oft to his frozen lair
Tracked I the grisly bear,
While from my path the hare
Fled like a shadow;
Oft through the forest dark
Followed the were-wolf's bark,
Until the soaring lark
Sang from the meadow.

"But when I older grew,
Joining a corsair's crew,
O'er the dark sea I flew
With the marauders.
Wild was the life we led;
Many the souls that sped,
Many the hearts that bled,
By our stern orders.

"Many a wassail-bout
Wore the long Winter out;
Often our midnight shout
Set the cocks crowing,

As we the Berserk's tale
Measured in cups of ale,
Draining the oaken pail,
Filled to o'erflowing.

"Once as I told in glee
Tales of the stormy sea,
Soft eyes did gaze on me,
Burning yet tender;
And as the white stars shine
On the dark Norway pine,
On that dark heart of mine
Fell their soft splendor.

"I wooed the blue-eyed maid,
Yielding, yet half afraid,
And in the forest's shade
Our vows were plighted.
Under its loosened vest
Fluttered her little breast,
Like birds within their nest
By the hawk frighted.

"Bright in her father's hall
Shields gleamed upon the wall,
Loud sang the minstrels all,
Chanting his glory;
When of old Hildebrand
I asked his daughter's hand,
Mute did the minstrels stand
To hear my story.

"While the brown ale he quaffed,
Loud then the champion laughed,
And as the wind-gusts waft
The sea-foam brightly,
So the loud laugh of scorn,
Out of those lips unshorn,
From the deep drinking-horn
Blew the foam lightly.

"She was a Prince's child,
I but a Viking wild,
And though she blushed and smiled,
I was discarded!
Should not the dove so white
Follow the sea-mew's flight,
Why did they leave that night
Her nest unguarded?

"Scarce had I put to sea,
Bearing the maid with me,
Fairest of all was she
Among the Norsemen!
When on the white sea-strand,
Waving his armèd hand,
Saw we old Hildebrand,
With twenty horsemen.

"Then launched they to the blast,
Bent like a reed each mast,
Yet we were gaining fast,
When the wind failed us;
And with a sudden flaw
Came round the gusty Skaw,
So that our foe we saw
Laugh as he hailed us.

"And as to catch the gale
Round veered the flapping sail,
'Death!' was the helmsman's hail,
'Death without quarter!'
Mid-ships with iron keel
Struck we her ribs of steel;
Down her black hulk did reel
Through the black water!

"As with his wings aslant,
Sails the fierce cormorant,
Seeking some rocky haunt,
With his prey laden,

So toward the open main,
Beating to sea again,
Through the wild hurricane,
Bore I the maiden.

"Three weeks we westward bore,
And when the storm was o'er,
Cloud-like we saw the shore
Stretching to leeward;
There for my lady's bower
Built I the lofty tower,
Which, to this very hour,
Stands looking seaward.

"There lived we many years;
Time dried the maiden's tears;
She had forgot her fears,
She was a mother;
Death closed her mild blue eyes,
Under that tower she lies;
Ne'er shall the sun arise
On such another!

"Still grew my bosom then,
Still as a stagnant fen!
Hateful to me were men,
The sunlight hateful!
In the vast forest here,
Clad in my warlike gear,
Fell I upon my spear,
Oh, death was grateful!

"Thus, seamed with many scars,
Bursting these prison bars,
Up to its native stars
My soul ascended!
There from the flowing bowl
Deep drinks the warrior's soul,
Skoal! to the Northland! skoal!"
Thus the tale ended.

Source: Longfellow, Henry Wadsworth. 1912. "The Skeleton in Armor." In *Yale Book of American Verse*, edited by Thomas R. Lounsbury. New Haven: Yale University Press. 99–109.

What Really Happened

Vikings throughout Scandinavia shared many important cultural features, which facilitated communication and movement between regions. However, the size of Scandinavia and the diverse types of landscape led to important regional differences in language, livelihood, culture, and routes of travel and trade. In addition, since the Scandinavian nations of today had barely begun to emerge, people of the time identified with a region rather than a nation, and conflict between different groups of Vikings was frequent (Price 2000, 118).

Between the third and sixth centuries, the language of Scandinavia was relatively unified and not very different from the language of most other Germanic-speaking areas in Europe. However, during the sixth, seventh, and eighth centuries, the language underwent drastic changes that separated the language of Scandinavia from its non-Nordic neighbors. Between the ninth and eleventh centuries, two major dialects begin to appear: Old West Norse (the language of Norway, the Faroe Islands, and Iceland) and Old East Norse (the language of Denmark and Sweden) (Haugen 1982, 9). In addition to these two main dialects, there was also a distinct dialect spoken on the island of Gotland off the eastern coast of Sweden called Old Gutnish. While the three dialects were mutually intelligible, there were significant differences in terms of pronunciation and morphology. It is hard to know exactly when the split began, since the only direct linguistic evidence comes from laconic runic inscriptions; the earliest vernacular manuscripts in Scandinavia are from Iceland and Norway and date from the mid-12th century.

Scandinavia is a large area. If Iceland is included, it runs from 55 degrees north into the Atlantic Ocean (a distance of more than 1,200 miles) and from the western top of Iceland at 24 degrees west of Greenwich to the eastern border of Norway and Finland at 31 degrees east. Accordingly, Vikings living in different regions took different routes when setting out on trading or raiding ventures. The Norse in the western part of Scandinavia and Denmark tended to sail westward to the British Isles or south to Germany, France, and Spain while the Norse in the eastern part—especially Sweden—ventured eastward to Finland, Estonia, Latvia, Russia, the Black and Caspian seas, and even as far as Byzantium. One characteristic of the Viking Age was the establishment of trading centers throughout Scandinavia, which included Hedeby, Birka, Kaupang, Ribe, and Århus, and additional centers or colonies within the Norse sphere of influence, such as Dublin, York, Wolin, Staraja Ladoga, Novgorod, and Kiev (Morris 2000, 100). In the trading colonies abroad, the Norse came into close contact with other cultures and inevitably assimilated, at least to some extent, into the native population.

The area outside of Scandinavia where the Norse exercised the most influence was the British Isles. Beginning with the attack on Lindisfarne in 793, Norwegian Vikings first raided English settlements and then focused on the Scottish Isles, such as the Shetland and Orkney Islands. In 834, the Danes began conducting summer raiding campaigns in England, but the raiders always returned home at the end of the season. However, in 850, Danish interests in England intensified, and for the first time, the Danish Vikings set up winter camp on the island of Thanet in the Thames, instead of returning to Denmark. From then on, the Danes controlled increasingly more land and often extracted tribute from the Anglo-Saxon population in exchange for being left in peace. The *Anglo-Saxon Chronicle* mentions such Danegeld (Danes' Pay) for the first time in 865. However, the very next year, in 866, what the *Anglo-Saxon Chronicle* calls the Great Heathen Army arrived in East Anglia and began to conquer large portions of the eastern part of England. After some twenty years of raids and battles, the borders of the Danelaw, the territories under Danish law, were established in a treaty in 885. After this, the Norse began to permanently settle in the Danelaw area and blended with the English population. The melding of Norse and English traditions is evident from stone carvings and other types of art. Place names with Norse elements like *-by* and *-thorpe* (as in Whitby, Balsy, Towthorpe, and Scunthorpe) are a testament to former Danish settlement areas in England. In addition, the English language was influenced through Anglo-Norse contact. For example, *window* from Old Norse *vindauga* (wind eye; window) and *take* from Old Norse *taka* (take) replaced earlier Old English *eyethurl* (window) and *niman* (take). Even the personal pronouns *they*, *them*, and *their* derive from Old Norse, replacing native *hīe/hēo*, *him/heom*, and *hira/heora* (Dawson 2003, 45).

On the route leading east, the Vikings established trading colonies in Russia, which later developed into cities, such as Kiev and Novgorod. Some runestones mention individuals who traveled to the east or the west. The most famous example of such a person is Ingvar the Far-Traveled, who lead an expedition to Persia. He is mentioned on at least 26 runestones in the eastern part of Sweden, raised in memory of his companions who died on the expedition (Thunberg 2010, 5). Some Norsemen traveling east also became part of the Varangian guard (see chapter 5). The Norse also quite literally left their mark in the east in the form of runic graffiti: the name Halfdan is legible in the mosque of Hagia Sophia in Constantinople (now Istanbul). In Sweden, evidence of cultural influence from the east abounds in the form of enormous quantities of Arab coins, lamellar armor (small iron plates sewn to a leather tunic instead of the interwoven rings forming chainmail) similar to those used in Russia found at Birka (Pedersen 2002, 33), and figures wearing eastern-style clothing—particularly pants with baggy legs popular in the Middle East for many centuries—are visible on some Gotlandic picture stones from the Viking Age (Nylén 1978, 90–94).

PRIMARY DOCUMENT

THE SAGA OF THE ORKNEY ISLANDERS (12TH–13TH CENTURY)

Orkneyinga saga (*the* Saga of the Orkney Islanders) *is an Old Norse-Icelandic saga composed by an anonymous Icelandic author at the end of the 12th century or the beginning of the 13th. Based on a combination of oral legend and written sources, it tells about the lives of the earls of Orkney. The extract below shows the close interaction between the Norse and inhabitants of Ireland and Scotland in both intermarriage with the nobility and military conflict. It also illustrates the mobility of the Norse during the Viking Age and the practice of summer Viking expeditions.*

11. Hlodver Thorfinn's son took the earldom after Ljot, and was a great chief; he had to wife Edna, daughter of Kjarval, the Irish king; their son was Sigurd the stout. Hlodver died of sickness, and is buried under a "how" at Hofn in Caithness. Sigurd, his son, took the earldom after him; he was a great chief and wide of lands. He held by main force Caithness against the Scots, and had a host out every summer. He harried in the Southern Isles, in Scotland and Ireland. It chanced one summer that Finnleik, the Scotearl, staked in a battle-field for Sigurd on Skidmoor by a day named, but Sigurd went to ask his mother's counsel, for she knew many things. The earl told her that there would not be less odds against him than seven men for one. She answers: "I had reared thee up long in my wool-bag had I known thou wouldest like to live for ever; and fate rules life, but not where a man is come; better it is to die with honour than to live with shame. Take thou

here hold of this banner which I have made for thee with all my cunning and I ween it will bring victory to those before whom it is borne, but speedy death to him who bears it." The banner was made with mickle needlecraft and famous skill. It was made in raven's shape; and when the wind blew out the banner, then it was as though the raven spread his wings for flight. Earl Sigurd was very wrath at the words of his mother, and gave the Orkneyingers their allodial holdings for their help, and so he fared to meet earl Finnleik on Skidmoor, and each drew up his host in battle array. And when the battle was joined, the banner bearer of earl Sigurd was shot to death. The earl bade another man go and bear the banner, and after they had fought a while that man fell. So three banner bearers of the earl fell, but he had the victory, and then the Orkneyingers got back their allodial rights.

12. Olaf Tryggvi's son was four years in warfare in the western lands since he had come from Vindland—the land of the Wends—ere he let himself be baptized in the Scilly isles. Thence he fared to England—read Ireland—and got there to wife Gyda, the daughter of Kvaran the Irish king. After that he stayed a while in Dublin until earl Hacon sent Thorir the whiner to lure him thence. Olaf sailed from the west with four ships and came first to the Orkneys. There he met earl Sigurd in Osmund's voe in South Rognvaldsey with three ships, and he was boun for warfare. King Olaf let the earl be called on board his ship and said he wished to talk with him; and when they met king Olaf spoke to him, "It is my will that thou lettest thyself be baptized and all the folk that serve thee, else thou shalt die here at once, but I will fare with fire and flame over all the isles." But when the earl saw into what a strait he had come he gave up all his suit into the king's power. The king then let him be baptized, and took as a hostage his son whose name was Hound or Whelp, but the king let him be baptized in the name of Hlodvir. Then all the Orkneys became Christian. But king Olaf then sailed east to Norway, and Hlodvir fared with him, but he lived a short while. But after that earl Sigurd yielded no obedience to king Olaf. He went into a marriage with a daughter of Malcolm the king of the Scots, and their son was earl Thorfinn. Earl Sigurd had before had three sons who were then alive, the name of one of them was Summerled, of the second Brusi, the third Einar.

13. A little while after the agreement between king Olaf and earl Sigurd Hlodversson, the earl took to wife the daughter of Malcolm, the Scot-king, and their son was earl Thorfinn. Earl Sigurd had three other sons, one was called Brusi, the second Summerled, the third Einar wry-mouth. Five winters after the battle at Svolder, earl Sigurd fared to Ireland, to help king Sigtrygg silk-beard, but he set up his elder sons over the lands, but

his son Thorfin, he gave over into the hands of the Scot-king, his mother's father, to foster. But when earl Sigurd came to Ireland, he and king Sigtrygg marched with that host to meet Brian, the Irish king, and their meeting was on Good Friday. Then it fell out that there was no one left to bear the raven banner, and the earl bore it himself, and fell there, but king Sigtrygg fled. King Brian fell with victory and glory.

14. After the fall of earl Sigurd, his sons took the realm and shared it into trithings among Summerled, Brusi, and Einar. Thorfinn was with the Scot-king five winters old when his father Sigurd fell. Then the Scot-king gave Thorfinn, his daughter's son, Caithness and Sutherland and the title of earl, and set up men to rule the land with him. Earl Thorfinn was early in coming to his full growth, the tallest and strongest of men; his hair was black, his features sharp, and his brows scowling, and as soon as he grew up it was easy to see that he was forward and grasping. Those brothers, Brusi and Einar, were unlike in temper. Einar was a man stern and grasping, unfriendly, and a mighty man for war. Brusi was a meek man, he kept his feelings well in hand and was humble, and ready-tongued. Summerled was like to Brusi in temper; he was the eldest of those brothers, and lived shortest, and died of sickness. After his death earl Thorfinn claimed a share of the realm in the Orkneys. Einar said that Thorfinn had Caithness and Sutherland, that realm which their father had owned, and called it more than a trithing of the isles, and would not grant Thorfinn a share after Summerled; but Brusi was willing to grant it, and gave over the share for his part. "I will not," he said, "covet more of the realm than that trithing which I own by right." Then Einar took two lots of the isles under him; then he made himself mighty, and had many followers, was oft a-warring in the summers, and had a great levy of men out of the land, but it was quite another story with the spoil. Then the freemen began to be weary of that toil; but the earl held boldly on with his burdens, and suffered no man to speak a word against him. Einar was the most overbearing of men. A great dearth arose in his realm from the toil and outgoings which the freemen had; but in that lot of the land that Brusi had was great peace and plenty, and the freemen had an easy life; for that he had many friends.

15. There was a powerful and wealthy man named Amund, he dwelt at Hrossey, at Sandwick on Lopness. His son's name was Thorkell, the properest man of all men who were then growing up in the Orkneys. Asmund was a wise man, and one of the men most esteemed in the islands. It fell out one spring that the earl had a mighty levy, as was his wont, but the freemen grumbled and took it ill, and brought the matter before Amund, and bade him speak to the earl for a little forbearance. Amund said the earl

would turn a deaf ear, "and little will come of it; as it is the earl and I are good friends, but methinks there is a great risk if we two should come to a quarrel with our tempers. No," says he, "I will have nothing to do with it." Then they told their story to Thorkell; he was loath to do anything, but still promised them his good offices, after being egged on by the men. Amund thought he had been too hasty in promising. But when the earl held a Thing, then Thorkell spoke on behalf of the freemen, told the need of the men, and bade the earl spare his people. Einarr answers well, and says he will give heed to his words: "I had meant now to have six ships out of the land, but now no more than three shall go; but as for thee, Thorkell, don't now ask this any more." The freemen thanked Thorkell well for his help. The earl fared away on a Viking voyage, and came back at autumn. But after that, in the spring, the earl had again a levy and held a Thing with the freemen. Then Thorkell spoke again, and bade the earl spare the freemen. The earl answers wrathfully, and said that the lot of the freemen should much worsen for his speech. He made himself so wood and wrath, that he said they should not be both there another spring safe and sound at the Thing. And so the Thing broke up. But when Amund became ware of what had passed between the earl and Thorkell, he begged Thorkell to go away. So he fared over to Caithness to earl Thorfinn, and was there long afterwards, and fostered him, when the earl was young, and was afterwards called Thorkell fosterer; and he was a man of mark. Many were the men of might who fled away out of the Orkneys for the overbearing of earl Einarr. Most fled to earl Thorfinn, some to Norway and to divers lands.

16. As soon as earl Thorfinn was grown up, then he sent a message to Einar his brother, and asked of him that share of the realm which he thought belonged to him in the Orkneys, but that was a trithing. Einar was in no hurry to lessen himself so. But when earl Thorfinn hears that, then he calls out force from Caithness. But when earl Einar was ware of that, then he gathers force, and goes against Thorfinn, and means to fight with him. Earl Brusi also gathers force, goes to meet them, and brings about an agreement that Thorfinn should have a trithing of the realm in the Orkneys which he owned by right, but earl Brusi and earl Einarr laid their lots together. Einar was to have the leadership over them, and the wardship of the land. But if either of them died before the other, then that one of them who lived longer should take the lands after the other. But that settlement was thought to be unfair, for Brusi had a son, whose name was Rognvald, but Einar was sonless. Earl Thorfinn sets men to keep watch and ward over that realm which he owned in the Orkneys; but he was most often in Caithness.

17. Earl Einar was most often in the summers in warfare round Ireland and Scotland and Wales. It happened one summer when he was warring on Ireland that he fought in Ulfreksfirth with Konufogur the Irish king. Earl Einar there got a mighty defeat and loss of men. The next summer after Eyvind Urarhorn fared from the west from Ireland, and meant to steer for Norway. The weather was sharp, and there was a great storm. Then Eyvind put in to Osmund's voe, and lay there weather bound a while. But when earl Einar learns that, then he went thither with a great force, and he took there Eyvind, and made them slay him, but gave peace to most of his men. They fared home to Norway about autumn, and went to find king Olaf, and told him how Eyvind had been taken off. The king answers little about it, and yet it could be found out that he thought this a mickle manscathe, and wrought more against himself than any one else. The king was short of words whenever he thought anything much against his mind. Earl Thorfinn sent Thorkell, his fosterer, out into the isles to get together his scatts and tolls. Earl Einar laid at Thorkell's door much of that rising against him which had happened when earl Thorfinn laid his claim out in the isles. Thorkell fared hastily out of the isles over to the Ness, and told earl Thorfinn that he had become sure of this, that earl Einar meant death for him, if his friends or kinsmen had not given him warning. "Now I must choose one of these two things, either to let the earl's and my meeting be so that we may settle our business once for all; or that other to fare further away, and thither where the earl shall never have power over me." Earl Thorfinn was very eager that he should fare east to Norway to meet King Olaf. "Thou wilt," says the earl, "be made much of wherever thou art with honourable men; but I know both your tempers, the earl's and thine, that ye two would be but a scant time before ye came to blows." Then Thorkell busked him to go to king Olaf, and fared about autumn to Norway, and was with king Olaf that winter in great love; the king took Thorkell much into his counsel. He thought, as was true, that Thorkell was a wise and very able man. The king found out from his talk that he was very uneven in his stories about the earls, and that he was a great friend of Thorfinn, but slow to praise earl Einar. And early next spring the king sent a ship west over the sea to find earl Thorfinn, and this bidding, by word of mouth, that the earl should come to see him. He did not lay the journey under his pillow, for words of friendship came along with the message.

Source: Dasent, George, trans. 1894. "The Orkneyingers Saga." In *Icelandic Sagas, and Other Historical Documents Relating to the Settlements and Descents of the Northmen on the British Isles*. Volume III. London: Her Majesty's Stationery Office. 14–21.

Further Reading

Barron, Elwyn A. 1888. *The Viking*. Chicago: A. C. McClurg and Company.

Dawson, Hope C. 2003. "Defining the Outcome of Language Contact: Old English and Old Norse." *OSUWPL* 57: 40–57.

Dennis, Andrew, Peter Foote, and Richard Perkins, trans. 1980. *Laws of Early Iceland: Grágás, the Codex Regius of Grágás, with Material from Other Manuscripts*. Winnipeg: University of Manitoba Press.

Haugen, Einar. 1982. *Scandinavian Language Structures: A Comparative Historical Survey*. Minneapolis: University of Minnesota Press.

Hochman, Adam. 2015. "Of Vikings and Nazis: Norwegian Contributions to the Rise and the Fall of the Idea of a Superior Aryan Race." *Studies in History and Philosophy of Biological Biomedical Sciences* 54: 84–88.

Morris, Christopher D. 2000. "The Viking Age in Europe." In *Vikings: The North Atlantic Saga*, edited by William W. Fitzhugh and Elisabeth I. Ward. Washington: Smithsonian Institution Press. 99–102.

Nylén, Erik. 1978. *Stones, Ships and Symbols: The Picture Stones of Gotland from the Viking Age and Before*. Stockholm: Gidlund.

Pedersen, Anne. 2002. "Scandinavian Weaponry in the Tenth Century: The Example of Denmark." In *A Companion to Medieval Arms and Armour: Swords of the Viking Age*, edited by David Nicolle. Rochester, NY: Boydell and Brewer. 25–35.

Pinkerton, John. 1798. *A Dissertation on the Origin and Progress of the Scythians or Goths: Being an Introduction to the Ancient and Modern History of Europe*. London: J. Nicols.

Price, Neil S. 2000. "Laid Waste, Plundered, and Burned: Vikings in Frankia." In *Vikings: The North Atlantic Saga*, edited by William W. Fitzhugh and Elisabeth I. Ward. Washington: Smithsonian Institution Press. 116–126.

Sturluson, Snorri. 1964. *Heimskringla: History of the Kings of Norway*, translated by Lee M. Hollander. Austin: Published for the American-Scandinavian Foundation by the University of Texas Press.

Swanton, Michael, trans. 2000. *The Anglo-Saxon Chronicles*. London: Phoenix Press.

Thunberg, Carl L. 2010. "Ingvarståget och dess monument. En studie av en runstensgrupp med förslag till ny gruppering." Bachelor's thesis. Göteborgs universitet. Accessed October 4, 2017. https://www.scribd.com/document/101948929/Thunberg-Carl-L-2010-Ingvarst%C3%A5get-och-dess-monument-En-studie-av-en-runstensgrupp-med-forslag-till-ny-gruppering.

Tveskov, Mark Axel, and Jon M. Erlandson. 2007. "Vikings, Vixens, and Valhalla." In *Box Office Archaeology: Refining Hollywood's Portrayals of the Past*, edited by Julie M. Schablitsky. Walnut Creek, CA: Left Coast. 34–50.

Whitelock, Dorothy, ed. 1979. *English Historical Documents, c. 500–1042*. Rev. ed. English Historical Documents. Volume 1. London: Eyre and Spottiswoode.

2

All Scandinavians Were Vikings

What People Think Happened

The word *Viking* was introduced into modern English in the 18th century, at which time it acquired the somewhat romanticized meaning "brutal warrior" or "noble barbarian." During the 20th century, the term was expanded to include not just those Scandinavian savages who suddenly appeared on foreign shores to plunder but also members of the culture that produced the voyaging raiders. This broad usage of the term *Viking* has irritated archaeologists, historians, and literary historians, though it is recognized that the etymology of the word *Viking* remains largely unresolved. One theory is that *Viking* derives from the Old Norse-Icelandic noun *vík* ("bay" or "creek"), in which case a Viking was someone who kept his ship in a bay for raiding or trading. Another theory is that the noun may be related to the place named Vik in southern Norway, which became an early center of Viking raiding fleets. A third theory is that the noun may be derived from the Old Norse-Icelandic verb *víkja*, in the meaning of "leaving home" or "departing." A fourth theory is that it may be a derivation of the Old English noun *wic* ("camp" or "trading place"), in which case a Viking was—according to the Anglo-Saxons—a warrior or a trader or maybe both. The most recent theory was advanced by Anatoly Liberman (2009), who examined the Old Norse-Icelandic noun *vika* ("sea mile") and the verb *víkja* in the sense of "turn." He draws attention to the fact that Viking ships were propelled with oars, arguing that "it is credible that the word for 'sea voyage, expedition' owes its existence to the idea of an oarsman's duty, the shift spent at the oars." His conclusion is that "A *víkingr* would then be someone on a rowing expedition. The occurrence of nearly the same word in Old Norse and Old English would also find a plausible explanation."

How the Story Became Popular

The idea that all Scandinavians were Vikings may at least in part be traced to non-Scandinavian, medieval accounts of the Scandinavian pirates. As noted in chapter 1, those medieval writers detailing the activities of the Vikings tended not to pay much attention to the heritage of their tormentors. Frankish sources refer to them as *Nordmanni* (Northmen), German sources as *Ascomanni* (Ashmen), Spanish sources as *al-Madjus* (heathen wizards), Slavic sources as *Rus* (the origin of the name has been debated), and Irish sources as *Lochlannach* (Northerners) or *Gaill* (Strangers) (Chartrand et al. 2006, 13). English sources generally refer to them as either pagans or Danes, even though not all the Vikings who showed up in England necessarily came from Denmark. In Old English, the word *wicing* first appears in the poem *Widsith*; the date of the poem has been disputed, but it may have been written in the seventh or ninth century.

In Scandinavia, the person credited with popularizing the word *Viking* and attaching it generally to the Scandinavian heritage is believed to be Erik Gustaf Geijer (1783–1847), a Swedish writer, historian, poet, philosopher, and musical composer. His poem *Vikingen* (*The Viking*), which portrayed the Viking as a heroic Norseman, and which appeared in the journal *Iduna* in 1811, did much to promote Swedish national romanticism and, by extension, the romanticized ideal of the Viking. Both Geijer and Esaias Tegnér (see chapter 1) were members of *Götiska förbundet* (The Geatish Society), a social club for literature studies among Swedish academics, which was founded by poets and authors in 1811, who sought to revive the so-called Viking spirit, and whose members would on occasion wear horned helmets (see chapter 9).

With the exception of historians, archaeologists, and literary historians, modern Scandinavians have not really made significant efforts to restrict the term to designate only those bands of men who plundered and colonized. In fact, Scandinavians use the Vikings as a kind of trademark. They seem to be proud of their Viking past and tend to look upon it as a golden age, a time when Scandinavia was in control of a sizeable portion of Europe. Some Scandinavians even use the term *Viking* to describe their heritage. The tourism and souvenir industry makes indiscriminate use of the word *Viking*. Reference may be made to Viking Cruises, Viking Airlines, and Hotel Viking. There are also Viking restaurants and Viking cafes. There is even such a thing as a Viking perfume, which was launched in 2017. The bottle features a Viking ship, and the perfume is advertised as follows:

> Viking, a fiery men's fragrance that bottles the fearless spirit of boundless exploration for the modern man who goes against the grain. Inspired by the incredibly crafted longships, a centerpiece of the Viking Age and one of the greatest design feats of the ninth century. A symbol of voyage and undeniable perseverance, longships were carefully designed for the skilled seaman who embodied unbridled determination to conquer. (Creed Boutique)

Interestingly, the nose behind the fragrance is not a Scandinavian nose but rather that of the French perfumer Olivier Creed.

PRIMARY DOCUMENT

ERIK GUSTAF GEIJER, *THE VIKING* (1811)

In 1811, Erik Gustaf Geijer's poem The Viking *was published and became very influential. The defeat suffered by the Swedes in 1809 through the loss of Finland to Russia caused him to become an extreme nationalist. In 1817, Geijer became professor of history at the University of Uppsala. His main academic works are* Svea rikes räfder *(1825;* The Annals of the Kingdom of Sweden*) and the three-volume* Svenska folkets historia *(1823–1826;* The History of the Swedes*).*

At fifteen the cabin grew close and confined.
Where we lived, my mother and I;
While tending the goats came a change o'er my mind,
As slowly the days crawled by.
In my dreams and my fancy I'd wonder and soar;
But I found not the joy that had cheered me before
In the woodland.

One morning a ship that I saw on the main
Like an arrow shot into our bay,
And my bosom heaved and my wants grew plain
To my fervid mind that day.

I left my mother, my goats and home
To join the Viking's crew and to roam.
O'er the ocean.

And the sails swell out, and lusty the wind
Bore us forth on the billows crest;
In the darkening sea sank the fields behind.
And yet there was joy in my breast.
I brandished my father's old broadsword on high
And swore to win booty and fame or to die
On the ocean.

At sixteen I slew the old Viking, for he
Made sport of my beardless chin.
I won trophies and glory as king of the sea,
In fierce fought battles and din.
I won castles and burghs on a foreign soil
And with my bold comrades cast lots for the spoil.
On the ocean.

And once even I possessed castles and lands
Where I quaffed by my sooty hearth-stone
And as ruler I looked to my country's demands
And I slept within walls of my own.
The days of the winter were dull to my mind;
'Tis true I was king, yet I yearned and I pined
For the ocean.

And time lagged idly and dull was my lot
To deal with the common herd;
They want me to watch o'er the peasant's cot
And the beggar's scrip to guard.
I listened all weary to cases and crimes.
And longed to go back to the gallant old times
On the ocean.

But the weary winter was ended at last,
And daisies grew bright on the shores;
And the wavelets chanted as on they passed,
Away where the ocean roars;

And spring winds gamboled o'er mountains and dale.
And the streams rush on with the speed of the gale
To the ocean.

I felt the invisible spirit of old

While the loud waves urged me on.
O'er city and country I scattered my gold;
My crown I trod upon.
With a ship and a sword and as poor as before
I courted new dangers and wrestled once more
With the ocean.

The wand was sportive and swift the chase
On the sea where'er we came,
But life and death of the human race
Was everywhere the same,
In human dwellings are grief and remorse
But sorrow, she knows not the Viking's course
On the ocean.

From the prow of the vessel my comrades and I
Scanned the restless seas again;
We would pass the merchant peacefully by
But fall on the Viking again.
For the Viking's laurels are dyed in blood
And their swords knit friendship and brotherhood
On the ocean.

I stood all the day in the bounding prow
And how bright the future smiled!
Like the swans where the tall reeds bend and bow,
I sped on the billows wild.
The booty that fell in my way was mine
And my hope was exalted as stars that shine
On the ocean.

And oft in the night as I watched alone
The elements fierce at strife,
I heard the fates in the storm and the moan.

As they spun out the thread of life.
His fall or his fortune man cannot control:
'Tis best be prepared amid billows that roll
On the ocean.

I am twenty now; I am wrecked and alone
And the sea cries loud for my blood.
He drank it in battles of days that are gone
Where I and my comrades stood;
Cease burning, my heart, and cease beating so loud
For soon thou'lt rest in thy watery shroud
In the ocean.

Thus sings the young Viking on desolate rock,
Ere, shipwrecked, he drowns as breakers attack
His perch and fiercely beset it.
The winds and the waves are changing their strain.
But the Viking's memory shall ever remain,
And the brave will never forget it.

Source: Geijer, Eric Gustav. 1896. "The Viking," translated by A. J. Pearson. *Progress* 2(5): 339–340.

What Really Happened

In Old Norse-Icelandic sources, the word *Viking* is not used about a people or a culture. *Víking* (a feminine noun) means a pirate raid. *Víkingr* (a masculine noun) refers to a man who participated in a pirate raid.

The fact of the matter is that not all Scandinavians were Vikings. The word *Viking* refers to a vocation and not an ethnic identity. There is, for example, no such thing as a Viking child or a Viking woman, although some evidence has been produced to testify to the existence of female Viking warriors. An example is the famous 10th-century Viking tomb, known as Bj 581 after its location when, in the 1880s, it was found and excavated on the island of Björkö, Sweden. The grave contained among other things a sword, an axe, two shields, skeletons of two horses, and the skeleton of a human being. On the basis of DNA tests and an analysis of isotopes of strontium, it has been argued that the skeleton was that of a woman. However, the argument has been rebutted in no uncertain words by, for example, Judith Jesch, who comments that "bones of various people might have gotten mixed together, given that 130 years have passed since the original excavation" (Christina Anderson 2017, A12). Else Roesdahl (1987) draws attention to the fact that Irish sources include mention of female warriors but comments that "these were probably dramatizations" (60). Her conclusion is that "[i]f female warriors did exist, they cannot have been many" (60).

Moreover, only a small number of men living in Scandinavia or the Norse islands engaged in Viking activity. The vast majority of men were ordinary and peaceful farmers, fishermen, hunters, merchants, craftsmen, carpenters, blacksmiths, or shipbuilders. Some of them also worked as lawyers, peacemakers, poets, and runecarvers. They all owed allegiance to a local chieftain or an earl, who in turn, at least in Denmark, Norway, and Sweden, owed allegiance to a king.

In addition, being a Viking seems to have been mostly a voluntary occupation or profession. It was an opportunity for a young man to get away from home, see and experience parts of the world, and make some money—a bit like what attracts young people to military service today.

There is, unfortunately, no contemporary complete biography of a Viking, but examples of the life of a Viking may be gleaned from short narratives detailing the activities of certain men in Old Norse-Icelandic medieval works. On such work is *Íslendingabók* (the *Book of Icelanders*) composed by Ari Thorgilsson in the beginning of the 12th century. It is told that two young Norwegian men, Ingolf and Hjorleif, spent some years on the high seas as Vikings and returned home as rich men. While in Norway, they got into trouble with the sons of a powerful earl and killed two of them in battle. As compensation, they had to give the earl all their land. Since there was no longer any land to be taken or bought in Norway, they made an exploratory expedition to Iceland, which at that time was unsettled and had only recently been discovered. They liked the island, so back home in Norway, they loaded their ships with domestic animals, food, and implements and sailed off to Iceland with their wives and children, free men, and slaves and settled. Hjorleif was killed in an uprising by his Irish slaves shortly after he had settled, but Ingolf and his household fared well. Ingolf eventually found a permanent settlement on the west coast of Iceland, where he lived as a farmer. He and his descendants were the ones who introduced legislation and brought about the unification of several small communities in their region with one local assembly.

Another work is *Göngu-Hrólfs saga* (the *Saga of Ganger-Hrolf*), a mythical heroic saga from the early 14th century. The eponymous hero of this saga is Hrolf, better known as Rollo, who began his life as a Viking but ended up as duke of Normandy, where he and his descendants ruled peacefully and kept the Vikings at bay (see chapter 5).

The examples of Ingolf, Hjorleif, and Hrolf show not only that some Vikings ended up as peaceful farmers, lawyers, or rulers after their adventures at sea but also that the word *Viking* should not be used consistently about a man who now and then participated in Viking raids. Being a Viking appears to have been a part-time profession, and a good example is provided by *Orkneyinga saga* (the *Saga of the Orkney Islanders*), an Icelandic work from the end of the 12th or the beginning of the 13th century. The saga relates that the Nordic chieftain Svein Asleifsson, a farmer in the Orkney Islands, raided twice a year in the Hebrides and Ireland. When in the spring he had carefully sowed seeds on his farm, he sailed off with five ships in order to plunder. He returned home to the Orkney Islands by the time the cornfields had been reaped and the grain had sprouted, and then he stayed for a while. In the late summer or early fall, he sailed off with seven ships and did not return until the first month of winter (Chartrand et al. 2006, 15–16).

The conclusion is that only a small portion of the male population of Scandinavia or places settled by Scandinavians, such as the Faroe Islands, the Orkney Islands, or Iceland, took part in raids on a regular basis. When a Viking abandoned activities associated with the Viking raids and returned home with his wealth and slaves, he was no longer a Viking. A man was a Viking only as long as he was on board a Viking ship and engaged in pillaging and plundering.

PRIMARY DOCUMENT

THE SAGA OF THE ORKNEY ISLANDERS (12TH–13TH CENTURY)

Orkneyinga saga *(the* Saga of the Orkney Islanders*) is an Old Norse-Icelandic saga composed by an anonymous Icelandic author at the end of the 12th century or the beginning of the 13th. Based on a combination of oral legend and written sources, it tells about the lives of the earls of Orkney. The extract below details the Viking habits of Svein Asleifsson.*

114. After the fall of earl Rognvald, earl Harold took all the isles under his rule, and became the sole chief over them. Earl Harold was a mighty chief, one of the tallest and strongest of men, "dour" and hard-hearted; he had to wife Afreka; their children were these: Henry and Hacon, Helena and Margaret. When Hacon was but a few winters old, Sweyn Asleif's son

offered to take him as his foster child, and he was bred up there, and as soon as ever he was so far fit, that he could go about with other men, then Sweyn had him away with him a sea roving every summer, and led him on to the worthiness in everything. It was Sweyn's wont at that time, that he sat through the winter at home in Gairsay, and there he kept always about him eighty men at his beck. He had so great a drinking hall, that there was not another as great in all the Orkneys. Sweyn had in the spring hard work, and made them lay down very much seed, and looked much after it himself. But when that toil was ended, he fared away every spring on a viking voyage, and harried about among the Southern isles and Ireland, and came home after midsummer. That he called spring-viking. Then he was at home until the corn fields were reaped down, and the grain seen to and stored. Then he fared away on a viking voyage, and then he did not come home till the winter was one month spent and that he called his autumn viking.

115. These tidings happened once on a time, that Sweyn Asleif's son fared away on his spring cruise, then Hacon earl Harold's son fared with him; and they had five ships with oars, and all of them large. They harried about among the Southern isles. Then the folk was so scared at him in the Southern isles, that men hid all their goods and chattels in the earth or in piles of rocks. Sweyn sailed as far south as Man, and got ill off for spoil. Thence they sailed out under Ireland and harried there. But when they came about south under Dublin, then two keels sailed there from off the main, which had come from England, and meant to steer for Dublin; they were laden with English cloths, and great store of goods was aboard them. Sweyn and his men pulled up to the keels, and offered them battle. Little came of the defence of the Englishmen before Sweyn gave the word to board. Then the Englishmen were made prisoners. And there they robbed them of every penny which was aboard the keels, save that the Englishmen kept the clothes they stood in and some food, and went on their way afterwards with the keels, but Sweyn and his men fared to the Southern isles, and shared their war spoil. They sailed from the west with great pomp. They did this as a glory for themselves when they lay in harbours, that they threw awnings of English cloth over their ships. But when they sailed into the Orkneys, they sewed the cloth on the fore part of the sails, so that it looked in that wise as though the sails were made altogether of broadcloth. This they called the broadcloth cruise. Sweyn fared home to his house in Gairsay. He had taken from the keels much wine and English mead. Now when Sweyn had been at home a short while, he bade to him earl Harold, and made a worthy feast

against his coming. When earl Harold was at the feast, there was much talk amongst them of Sweyn's good cheer. The earl spoke and said: "This I would now, Sweyn, that thou wouldest lay aside thy sea rovings; 'tis good now to drive home with a whole wain. But thou knowest this, that thou hast long maintained thyself and thy men by sea roving, but so it fares with most men who live by unfair means, that they lose their lives in strife, if they do not break themselves from it." Then Sweyn answered, and looked to the earl, and spoke with a smile, and said thus: "Well spoken is this, lord, and friendly spoken, and it will be good to take a bit of good counsel from you; but some men lay that to your door, that ye too are men of little fairness." The earl answered: "I shall have to answer for my share, but a gossiping tongue drives me to say what I do." Sweyn said: "Good, no doubt, drives you to it, lord. And so it shall be, that I will leave off sea roving, for I find that I am growing old, and strength lessens much in hardships and warfare. Now I will go out on my autumn cruise, and I would that it might be with no less glory than the spring cruise was; but after that my warfaring shall be over." The earl answers: "'Tis hard to see, messmate, whether death or lasting luck will come first." After that they dropped talking about it. Earl Harold fared away from the feast, and was led out with fitting gifts. So he and Sweyn parted with great love-tokens.

116. A little after Sweyn busks him for his roving cruise; he had seven longships and all great. Hacon earl Harold's son went along with Sweyn on his voyage. They held on their course first to the Southern isles, and got there little war spoil; thence they fared out under Ireland, and harried there far and wide. They fared so far south as Dublin, and came upon them there very suddenly, so that the townsmen were not ware of them before they had got into the town. They took there much goods. They made prisoners there those men who were rulers in the town. The upshot of their business was that they gave the town up into Sweyn's power, and agreed to pay as great a ransom as he chose to lay upon them. Sweyn was also to hold the town with his men and to have rule over it. The Dublin men swear an oath to do this. They fared to their ships at even, but next morning Sweyn was to come into the town, and take the ransom, place his men about the town, and take hostages from the townsmen. Now it must be told of what happened in the town during the night. The men of good counsel who were in the town held a meeting among themselves, and talked over the straits which had befallen them; it seemed to them hard to let their town come into the power of the Orkneyingers, and worst of all

of that man whom they knew to be the most unjust man in the Western lands. So they agreed amongst themselves that they would cheat Sweyn if they might. They took that counsel, that they dug great trenches before the burg gate on the inside, and in many other places between the houses where it was meant that Sweyn and his men should pass; but men lay in wait there in the houses hard by with weapons. They laid planks over the trenches, so that they should fall down as soon as ever a man's weight comes on them. After that they strewed straw on the planks so that the trenches might not be seen, and so bided the morrow.

117. On the morning after Sweyn and his men arose and put on their arms; after that they went to the town. And when they came inside beyond the burg gate the Dublin men made a lane from the burg gate right to the trenches. Sweyn and his men saw not what they were doing, and ran into the trenches. The townsmen they ran straightway to hold the burg gate, but some to the trenches, and brought their arms to bear on Sweyn and his men. It was unhandy for them to make any defence, and Sweyn lost his life there in the trenches, and all those who had gone into the town. So it was said that Sweyn was the last to die of all his messmates, and spoke these words ere he died: "Know this all men, whether I lose my life today or not, that I am one of the saint earl Rognvald's bodyguard, and I now mean to put my trust in being there where he is with God." Sweyn's men fared at once to their ships and pulled away, and nothing is told about their voyage before they come into the Orkneys. There now is an end of telling about Sweyn; and it is the talk of men that he hath been most of a man for his own sake in the Western lands, both of yore and now a days, of those men who had no higher titles of honour than he.

After the fall of Sweyn, his sons Olaf and Andrew shared his inheritance between them. They made the next summer after Sweyn lost his life a party-wall in that great drinking hall which he had owned in Gairsay. Andrew Sweyn's son had to wife Frida Kolbein the burly's daughter, sister of Bjarni, bishop of the Orkneyingers.

Earl Harold now ruled over the Orkneys, and was the greatest chief; he had to wife afterwards Hvarflada earl Malcolm's daughter of Moray. Their children were these: Thorfinn, David, and John, Gunhilda, Herborga, and Longlife.

Source: Vigfusson, Gudbrand, ed., and George W. Dasent, trans. 1887. *Icelandic Sagas and Other Historical Works Relating to the Settlements and Descents of the Northmen on the British Isles*, 4 vols., rolls series 88. Volume 3. London: Eyre and Spottiswoode. 220–224.

Further Reading

Anderson, Christina. 1997. "A Female Viking Warrior? A Tomb Yields Clues." *The New York Times*, September 18. A12.

Chartrand, R., K. Durham, M. Harrison, and I. Heath. 2006. *The Vikings: Voyagers of Discovery and Plunder*. Foreword by Magnus Magnusson. Oxford: Osprey Publishing.

Creed Boutique. "Creed Viking." Accessed October 1, 2017. https://www.creedboutique.com/men/269-viking-.html.

Liberman, Anatoly. 2009. "What Did the Vikings Do Before They Began to Play Football?" July 15. Accessed September 28, 2017. http://blog.oup.com/2009/07/vikings/.

Roesdahl, Else. 1986. *The Vikings*, translated by Susan M. Margeson and Kirsten Williams. London: Penguin Press.

Swanton, Michael, ed. and trans. 2000. *The Anglo-Saxon Chronicles*. London: Phoenix Press.

3

Vikings Were Barbarians

What People Think Happened

The erroneous idea that Vikings were barbarians has several components that are treated in other chapters; examples include the skull cups (chapter 11), the primitive weapons (chapter 7), the carving of the blood eagle (chapter 10), and the idea that they were filthy (chapter 8). Despite the refutation of these ideas, the notion still persists that Vikings were uncultured. This misconception may be traced to the 18th century.

In 18th-century England, neoclassicism was in vogue, and Greco-Roman literature, art, and architecture were revered for their classical values of balance and rationalism. Paintings and sculptures imitated the style of classical art, and religious and government buildings inspired by Greek and Roman temples sprang up all over Europe. Alongside neoclassicism, the romantic movement grew, the interest of which lay contrary to neoclassical values. The focus of this movement was emotion—the irrational, the terrible, and the awe-inspiring, which is known as the sublime. Rather than identifying their cultural roots with ancient Greece and Rome, romantics looked to the Germanic tribes and their achievements as their cultural forebears. To many intellectuals of the 18th century, Germanic and especially Norse culture was seen as embodying the antithesis of Greco-Roman values and decorum (Fjalldal 2015, 327). The Vikings were equated with other ancient Germanic tribes such as the Goths, who had caused the downfall of the Roman Empire. They were those "whose furious ravages destroyed the last poor remains of expiring genius among the Romans" (Percy 1763, A2). Proponents of neoclassicism were not friendly toward the interest of their romantic peers in northern arts and literature. In a letter to Earl George

Montagy, Horace Walpole expressed his opinion of the work of Thomas Gray (1716–1771) with Old Norse poetry: "Who can care through what horrors a Runic savage arrived at all the joys and glories they could conceive, the supreme felicity of boozing ale out of the skull of an enemy in Odin's hall?" (Cunningham 1891, 91). Walpole's opinion was shared by others, who believed that Norse literature and culture were the works of primitive savages, especially in comparison to the achievements of the Greeks and Romans. In his preface to *Five Pieces of Runic Poetry Translated from the Islandic Language* (1763), Thomas Percy sums up a common European opinion of the Norse during his time: "The ancient inhabitants of the northern parts of Europe are generally known under no other character than that of a hardy and unpolished race, who subdued all the southern nations by a dint of courage and of numbers" (A2).

How the Story Became Popular

During the 17th century, a number of Old Norse-Icelandic texts were brought from Iceland to Europe, where they were translated by antiquarians into Latin and occasionally modern Nordic languages. However, it was not until the mid-18th century that these texts truly became of interest to non-Scandinavian scholars, though the reception of the texts varied. Eighteenth-century translations into modern European languages were mostly translations of 17th-century Latin translations by Nordic scholars. Since the poems chosen by these early Nordic scholars often concerned death and other terrifying events, the general European perception of the Old Norse literary corpus—and by extension, the Vikings—became skewed (Gylfi Gunnlaugsson 2009, 92–93). Thomas Percy, too, was under the impression that Old Norse-Icelandic literature was particularly grim; in the preface to his *Five Pieces of Runic Poetry* he writes that "[f]rom the following specimens it will be found, that the poetry of the Scalds chiefly displays itself in images of terror" (A6). An example is the skaldic poem *Krákumál* (the *Lay of Kraka*), in which Ragnar Shaggy-Breeches describes his brutal battles against King Ella and at the end laughs in the face of his own death. The mistranslation of a kenning (poetic circumlocution), which resulted in the faulty idea that Vikings drank out of the skulls of their enemies (see chapter 11), certainly added to the perceived grim character of the Norsemen. The other selections of Old Norse-Icelandic poetry and literature that had been translated dealt with mythological subjects, with the result that medieval Scandinavian literature was considered to embody the terrible and sublime by early romantics (Clunies Ross and Lönnroth 1999, 16).

In addition to being thought of as sublime, the Vikings were perceived of by the romantics as noble savages. The Romantic Movement was influenced by, for example, Jean-Jacques Rousseau's (1712–1778) *Discours sur l'origine et les fondements de l'inégalité parmi les hommes* (1755, *Discourse on the Origin and Basis of Inequality Among Men*), which advanced the idea that humans were basically good in their natural state before becoming civilized and corrupted (Cranston 2017). Accordingly, the Vikings were regarded as a primitive people largely unspoiled by civilization at the northern extreme of Europe and far from the influence of Rome. Percy expresses this sentiment in the prologue to his translation of Old Norse-Icelandic poetry, which he considers to be "the workings of the human mind in its almost original state of nature" (A8). The reception of the Vikings during the 18th century was thus mixed. Those who adhered to classical values and aesthetics believed that the Norse were barbarians, whose greatest achievement was excelling in brutality, while those interested in literature and culture considered them to be primitive, noble savages uncorrupted by civilization. However, in both cases, the Vikings were perceived as uncivilized—positive or negative.

During the 19th century, the national romantic movement intensified especially among the English, Germans, Dutch, and naturally, the Scandinavians, who all looked to the Nordic past (Clunies Ross and Lönnroth 1999, 18). Although by the end of the century, many artists and intellectuals began to reject romanticism and lost interest in Norse culture, the wider public still remained fascinated with Vikings, and in the early 20th century, the Vikings made their appearance on the silver screen. In the silent film *The Viking* (1928), for example, there is a scene in which the Vikings attack the castle of the Earl of Northumbria and take him prisoner. Here they are depicted as the epitome of the image of the barbarian: a wild horde with unkempt hair and beards, clad in rough furs and horned helmets, storming the castle, a symbol of civilization. In the influential Hollywood film *The Vikings* (1958), the Norse are shown as violent ruffians who hold raucous feasts and pursue pleasures with reckless abandon. Several of the scenes in the film even had to be cut from the final version because they were deemed too brutal or sexually explicit by the Product Code Administration (PCA), Hollywood's self-censorship system (Kelly 2011, 13–14). However, some scenes the PCA objected to as excessively brutal, such as the blinding of Einar by a hawk and the amputation and cauterizing of Erik's hand, remained, because the producer, Jerry Bresler, successfully argued that they were essential to the plot. The film *Valhalla Rising* (2009) brings brutality to new heights. The main character is a muscular, mute, one-eyed Norse warrior known as "One Eye," who is held captive by Scottish highlanders like a wild animal and periodically released to fight other similarly captive Norsemen. One Eye's wordless existence, grim presence, and brutal fighting style lend him an animalistic quality, and it would be hard to imagine an even more barbarian Viking character than him.

The world of video games has also been enamored with the idea of Vikings as barbarians. Fantasy role-playing games often include a "barbarian" character, who is often loosely or overtly based on Vikings, while other games place more focus on Norse themes than others. One example is the game "For Honor" (2017), which features three different factions or ethnic groups to choose from: European knights, Japanese samurai, and Norse Vikings. In the Viking faction, players choose between characters called Highlander, Raider, Warlord, Berserker, and Valkyrie. Both the Valkyrie and Raider characters wear horned helmets, all the male characters sport formidable beard styles, and the Raider has several human bones dangling from his belt. The overall impression of the Vikings in "For Honor" is that of fierce, brutal warriors, utterly fearless of death, much in the spirit of Ragnar laughing at his own death in *Krákumál*. While it is true that the Vikings were fearsome warriors, they were also advanced in terms of technology and art, as demonstrated below.

PRIMARY DOCUMENT

PAUL HENRI MALLET'S *NORTHERN ANTIQUITIES* (1756)

This excerpt from Thomas Percy's translation of Paul Henri Mallet's Northern Antiquities, or, An Historical Account of the Manners, Customs, Religion and Laws, Maritime Expeditions and Discoveries, Language and Literature of the Ancient Scandinavians, *revised by I. A. Blackwell, emphasizes the warlike nature of the Vikings and their excessive drinking. The Scandinavians were supposedly so stubbornly adherent to their drinking, in particular to their heathen gods, such that early missionaries decided it would be easier to change the objects of their toasts to God, Jesus, and the saints, rather than attempting to stop the practice entirely. This description exemplifies and perpetuates the 18th- and 19th-century European view of the Norse as less-cultured and impulsive barbarians.*

Whoever attempts to delineate the manners of the ancient inhabitants of the north, will find their love of war and passion for arms amongst the most characteristic and expressive lines of the portrait. Their prejudices, their customs, their daily occupations, their amusements, in short, every action of their lives, were all impressed with this passion. They passed the greatest part of their time either in camps or on board their fleets, employed in real engagements, in preparations for them, or in sham fights; for whenever they were constrained to live in peace, the resemblance of war furnished out their highest entertainment. They then had reviews, mock battles, which frequently ended in real ones, tournaments, the bodily exercises of wrestling, boxing, racing, etc. The rest of their time was commonly spent in hunting, public business, drinking and sleeping. "The Germans," says Tacitus, "when not engaged in war, pass their time in indolence, feasting and sleep. The bravest and most warlike among them do nothing themselves; but transfer the whole care of the house, family and possessions to the females, the old men and such as are infirm among them: and the same people, by a strange contradiction of nature, both love inaction and hate peace." All the Celtic nations lie under the same reproach from the Greek and Roman authors; and it is easy to conceive, that a people who affixed ideas of contempt to all labour of body and mind, had for the most part nothing else to do but to carouse and sleep, whenever the state did not call them to arms. This was the badge and noblest privilege of their liberty; every free man placed his glory and happiness in being often invited to solemn entertainments; and the hopes of partaking of eternal feasts filled, as we have seen, the north with heroes. Other pleasures and other rewards have been conceived under the influence of other climes: all nations have in their infancy been governed by the force of climate; and their first legislators, far from endeavouring to stem this torrent, but borne away with it themselves, have ever by their laws and institutions enlarged and increased its natural prevalence. We find remarkable instances in the Icelandic Sagas of frequent and excessive feastings. Tacitus observes, that the plentiful tables of the chiefs, were, among the Germans, the wages of their dependents. Nor could a great lord or chieftain take a readier way to attract a numerous train of followers, than by often making magnificent entertainments. It was at table that the Germans consulted together on their most important concerns, such as the electing of their princes, the entering into war, or the concluding of peace, &c. On the morrow they re-considered the resolutions of the preceding night, supposing, adds the same historian, "that the proper time to take each other's opinions was when the soul was too open for disguise; and to determine, when it was too cautious to err." The common liquors at these carousals were either beer, mead, or wine, when they could get it: these they drank out of earthen or wooden pitchers, or else out of the horns of wild bulls, with which their forests abounded. The principal person at the table took the cup first, and rising up, saluted by name either him who sat next him, or him who was nearest in rank; then he drank it off, and causing it to be filled up again to the brim, presented it to the man whom he had saluted. Hence came the custom of drinking to the health of the guests: but I know not whether that of drinking to the honour of the gods was generally practised among all the Teutonic people, or only among the Scandinavians. Snorri Sturlason says, " that in the solemn festivals, such as usually followed the sacrifices, they emptied what was called the cup of Odin, to obtain victory and a glorious reign; then the cups of Njörd and of Frey, for a plentiful season; after which several used to take off another to Bragi, the God of Eloquence and Poetry." The Scandinavians were so much addicted to this custom, that the first missionaries, unable to abolish it, were forced instead of these false deities to substitute the true God, Jesus Christ, and the saints; to whose honour they devoutly drank for many ages. In the pagan times, they also drank to the heroes, and to such of their friends as had fallen bravely in battle. Lastly, it was at these feasts, for the most part, that those associations were formed and confirmed which the old chronicles so often mention. There was scarcely a valiant man who was not a member of one or more of these societies; the chief tie of which was a solemn obligation entered into, to defend and protect their companions on all occasions, and to revenge their deaths at the hazard of their own lives. This oath was taken and renewed at their festivals, which had also their respective laws. Fraternities of this sort still subsisted after the Christian religion was received in the north, but by degrees the object was changed. When the harbouring projects of enmity and revenge were for bidden at them, these meetings had no other object or support but drunkenness and intemperance. More than two hundred years after the Scandinavians had embraced Christianity there were still confraternities of which the first nobility were members. But the disorders committed at these meetings increasing, the Councils were at last obliged to suppress them.

Source: Mallet, Paul Henri. 1847. *Northern Antiquities, or, An Historical Account of the Manners, Customs, Religion and Laws, Maritime Expeditions and Discoveries, Language and Literature of the Ancient Scandinavians*, edited by I. A. Blackwell, translated by Thomas Percy. London: Bohn. 194–198.

What Really Happened

The Vikings were, in many ways, technologically advanced for their time, especially in the areas of maritime technology, fortress building, art, and poetry. Shipbuilding was arguably the height of Norse technology and allowed the Vikings to trade and raid from Western Europe to the Black and Caspian Seas. Evidence of Viking ships comes from archaeological finds in Norway, Denmark, and Sweden, and from carvings on picture stones and other visual representations. A variety of types of ships existed, ranging from small vessels that could be rowed by a single person to large cargo ships and narrow, fast warships. Scandinavian vessels were clinker built, with rows of overlapping strakes or planks, and held together by ribs spanning across the inside of the hull for stability. Ships were equipped with a keel, a side rudder, a mast, and a square sail, and could be rowed with oars for additional speed or in the absence of wind. The low draft of Viking ships allowed the Norse to travel up shallow rivers, and they could also be carried over land between rivers.

The two best-preserved ships from Viking Age Scandinavia are the Gokstad and Oseberg ships from the Oslo Fjord in Norway. The early-ninth-century Oseberg ship is the most famous. It appears not to have been an oceangoing vessel, but rather a luxury yacht used for local travel within fjords and coastal areas. Its stems are ornately carved with interlocking gripping beasts and terminate in carved spirals. The lavish decoration indicates that the ship belonged to a very high-status individual. The Gokstad ship dates from the late ninth or early 10th century and is much more seaworthy than the Oseberg ship. The vessel is 78.1 feet long and over 16.7 feet wide, though true warships were narrower in proportion for greater speed and maneuverability. Cargo ships were wider and deeper than warships and general transport ships to accommodate a larger volume of goods. The ship *Skuldelev 1*, discovered in the Roskildefjord in Denmark, is a cargo ship over 53.5 feet long and 14.8 feet wide, with a loading capacity of almost 27 tons (Roesdahl 1991, 89–90). The hull is higher than those of the Gokstad and Oseberg ships, rendering it suitable for travel on the rough seas of the North Atlantic.

Another area in which Vikings excelled is the building of fortifications. Fortresses have been built in Scandinavia since the Iron Age and were either situated on hilltops—taking advantage of natural barriers such as marshes or cliffs—or on flat ground. One such ring fort is Eketorp, on the Swedish island Öland, which was first built between 300 and 400; after its rebuilding around 1100, it was enclosed by two ring walls with an inner diameter of about 80 meters (Wolf 2004, 93). In addition, many towns had fortifications. Examples include Birka, Hedeby, Århus, and Västergarn. Some fortifications were intended as refuge camps, the largest of which is Torsburg on Gotland, which is situated on a plateau, protected by 1.24 miles of wall, and could have accommodated the entire population of the island with their animals and fodder in times of danger (Roesdahl 1991, 130–131).

The most impressive ring forts are found in Denmark and date from the late 10th century. The four fortresses of this type at Trelleborg, Aggersborg, Fyrkat, and Nonnebakken were probably built by King Harald Bluetooth (d. ca. 986). Their layout is perfectly circular, with four gates, one at each compass point. The largest of these ring forts is Aggersborg, which, with its inner diameter of around 787.4 feet, would have accommodated about 3,000 people (Wolf 2004, 91–92). Still another feat of Viking Age engineering is the Danevirke (Defense of the Danes), a network of earthwork ramparts spanning across the southern border of the Jutland Peninsula between Hedeby by the Schlei Fjord and the rivers Treene and Rheide. The complex was constructed beginning in 737 as a protection from the Danes' neighboring Saxons, Frisians, and Slavs (Roesdahl 1991, 133). The Danevirke spans about 18.6 miles in total, making it one of the most impressive defensive structures of Viking Age Scandinavia (Wolf 2004, 93–94).

The Norse were also highly sophisticated in terms of art and literature. An area of visual art in which Vikings truly excelled was woodcarving. In addition to the ostentatiously carved Oseberg ship, many other artifacts were found at the burial site, such as carved animal heads, a wooden carriage, a sled, and a bedframe, which demonstrate considerable artistic skill. The pinnacle of Viking woodcarving is likely the 12th-century Urnes stave church in Norway, from which the last style of Viking art takes its name. The most elaborate carvings in the church surround the door in the north wall and depict a stag with elongated proportions, completely intertwined in serpents and plant tendrils. Viking Age Scandinavians also carved in stone and left behind about 3,000 runestones, many of which had pictorial decorations in addition to runic script. The Urnes style appears on runestones in the mid-11th century and manifests itself in terms of serpents (whose bodies contain the runic inscription) with characteristic elongated, almond-shaped eyes. The island of Gotland had its own tradition of carving picture stones, which began in the fifth century and carried on in various styles through the 12th century. Many picture stones depict a rider on horseback (who has been interpreted as Odin on his eight-legged horse, Sleipnir, in some cases) greeted by a female figure bearing a drinking horn.

Poetry was an important part of Viking Age culture and is divided into two categories: eddic and skaldic poetry. Eddic poetry has been preserved mainly in the *Codex Regius* (the *King's Book*) from the late 13th century (see chapter 4), although most of the poems were likely composed much earlier (Jónas Kristjánsson 1997, 28). A few runestones with poetry in the same meter as most eddic poetry have been found, such as the Swedish

Rök and Högby runestones (Ög 136 and Ög 81), dating from around 800 and the early 11th century, respectively. The earliest example of skaldic poetry is found on the Karlevi runestone (Öl 1) from the late 10th century on the Swedish island of Öland. Skaldic poetry was composed primarily for chieftains and kings to commemorate their achievements. It typically uses the meter known as *dróttkvætt* (courtly meter), which has a very sophisticated and complicated alliteration and rhyme scheme. In addition, it makes extensive use of poetic circumlocutions known as kennings, such as *whale-road* to mean *ocean*, or *feeder of ravens* to mean *warrior*.

Considering their highly advanced technological and artistic skills, the Vikings cannot be considered primitive.

PRIMARY DOCUMENT

EGILL SKALLA-GRÍMSSON, *SONATORREK* (CA. 910–990)

The following poem, known as Sonatorrek (Sons' Loss) *was composed by Egill Skalla-Grímsson (ca. 910–990), and is recorded in some manuscripts of* Egils saga Skalla-Grímssonar (the Saga of Egil Skalla-Grimsson). *Although the saga itself was written at least two centuries after Egill's life, scholars accept the poem's attribution to him. According to the saga, Egill composed the poem after the death of his son Böðvar at the encouragement of his daughter, in order to distract him from starving himself to death out of grief. In the poem, Egill laments the loss of both his sons, his loss of trust in Odin, but while composing the poem, he is able to overcome his grief.*

1.
'Much doth it task me
My tongue to move,
Through my throat to utter
The breath of song.
Poesy, prize of Odin,
Promise now I may not,
A draught drawn not lightly
From deep thought's dwelling.

2.
'Forth it flows but hardly;
For within my breast

Heaving sobbing stifles
Hindered stream of song
Blessed boon to mortals
Brought from Odin's kin,
Goodly treasure, stolen
From Giant-land of yore.

3.
'He, who so blameless
Bore him in life,
O'erborne by billows
With boat was whelmed.
Sea-wavesflood that whilom
Welled from giant's wound
Smite upon the grave-gate
Of my sire and son.

4.
'Dwindling now my kindred
Draw near to their end,
Ev'n as forest-saplings
Felled or tempest-strown.
Not gay or gladsome
Goes he who beareth
Body of kinsman
On funeral bier.

5.
'Of father fallen
First I may tell;
Of much-loved mother
Must mourn the loss.
Sad store hath memory
For minstrel skill,
A wood to bloom leafy
With words of song.

6.
'Most woful the breach,
Where the wave in-brake

On the fenced hold
Of my father's kin.
Unfilled, as I wot,
And open doth stand
The gap of son rent
By the greedy surge.

7.
'Me Ran, the sea-queen,
Roughly hath shaken:
I stand of beloved ones
Stript and all bare.
Cut hath the billow
The cord of my kin,
Strand of mine own twisting
So stout and strong.

8.
'Sure, if sword could venge
Such cruel wrong,
Evil times would wait Ægir, ocean-god.
That wind-giant's brother
Were I strong to slay,
'Gainst him and his sea-brood
Battling would I go.

9.
'But I in no wise
Boast, as I ween,
Strength that may strive
With the stout ships' Bane.
For to eyes of all
Easy now 'tis seen
How the old man's lot
Helpless is and lone.

10.
'Me hath the main
Of much bereaved;
Dire is the tale,

The deaths of kin:
Since he the shelter
And shield of my house
Hied him from life
To heaven's glad realm.

11.
'Full surely I know,
In my son was waxing
The stuff and the strength
Of a stout-limbed wight:
Had he reached but ripeness
To raise his shield,
And Odin laid hand
On his liegeman true.

12.
'Willing he followed
His father's word,
Though all opposing
Should thwart my rede:
He in mine household
Mine honour upheld,
Of my power and rule
The prop and the stay.

13.
'Oft to my mind
My loss doth come,
How I brotherless bide
Bereaved and lone.
Thereon I bethink me,
When thickens the fight
Thereon with much searching
My soul doth muse:

14.
'Who staunch stands by me
In stress of fight,
Shoulder to shoulder,

Side by side?
Such want doth weaken
In war's dread hour;
Weak-winged I fly,
Whom friends all fail.

15.
'Son's place to his sire
(Saith a proverb true)
Another son born
Alone can fill.
Of kinsmen none
(Though ne'er so kind)
To brother can stand
In brother's stead.

16.
'O'er all our ice-fields,
Our northern snows,
Few now I find
Faithful and true.
Dark deeds men love,
Doom death to their kin,
A brother's body
Barter for gold.

17.
'Unpleasing to me
Our people's mood,
Each seeking his own
In selfish peace.
To the happier bees' home
Hath passed my son,
My good wife's child
To his glorious kin.

18.
'Odin, mighty monarch,
Of minstrel mead the lord,
On me a heavy hand

Harmful doth lay.
Gloomy in unrest
Ever I grieve,
Sinks my drooping brow,
Seat of sight and thought.

19.
'Fierce fire of sickness
First from my home
Swept off a son
With savage blow:
One who was heedful,
Harmless, I wot,
In deeds unblemished,
In words unblamed.

20.
'Still do I mind me,
When the Friend of men
High uplifted
To the home of gods
That sapling stout
Of his father's stem,
Of my true wife born
A branch so fair.

21.
'Once bare I goodwill
To the great spear-lord,
Him trusty and true
I trowed for friend:
Ere the giver of conquest,
The car-borne god,
Broke faith and friendship
False in my need.

22.
'Now victim and worship
To Vilir's brother,
The god once honoured,

I give no more.
Yet the friend of Mimir
On me hath bestowed
Some boot for bale,
If all boons I tell.

23.
'Yea he, the wolf-tamer,
The war-god skilful,
Gave poesy faultless
To fill my soul:
Gave wit to know well
Each wily trickster,
And force him to face me
As foeman in fight.

24.
'Hard am I beset;
Whom Hela, the sister
Of Odin's fell captive,
On Digra-ness waits.
Yet shall I gladly
With right good welcome
Dauntless in bearing
Her death-blow bide.'

Source: Green, W. C., trans. 1893. *The Story of Egil Skallagrímsson: Being an Icelandic Family History of the Ninth and Tenth Centuries.* London: E. Stock. 171–174.

Further Reading

Clunies Ross, Margaret, and Lönnroth, Lars. 1999. "The Norse Muse: Report from an International Research Project." *Alvíssmál* 9: 3–28.

Cranston, Maurice. 2017. "Jean-Jacques Rousseau." *Encyclopædia Britannica.* Accessed October 20, 2017. https://www.britannica.com/biography/Jean-Jacques-Rousseau.

Cunningham, Peter, ed. 1891. *The Letters of Horace Walpole.* Volume 5. London: Richard Bentley and Son.

Fjalldal, Magnús. 2015. "The Last Viking Battle." *Scandinavian Studies* 87(3): 317–331.

Foote, Peter, and David M. Wilson. 1970. *The Viking Achievement: The Society and Culture of Early Medieval Scandinavia*. London: Sidgwick & Jackson.

Gunnlaugsson, Gylfi. 2009. "Taming the Barbarian: Literary Representations of Northern Antiquity, 1750–1850." *Scandia* 75(2): 91–97.

Kelly, Kathleen Coyne. 2011. "The Trope of the Scopic in *The Vikings* (1958)." In *The Vikings on Film: Essays on Depictions of the Nordic Middle Ages*, edited by Kevin J. Harty. Jefferson, NC: McFarland & Company.

Kristjánsson, Jónas. 1997. *Eddas and Sagas: Iceland's Medieval Literature*. Reykjavík: Hið íslenska bókmenntafélag.

Nylén, Erik. 1978. *Stones, Ships and Symbols: The Picture Stones of Gotland from the Viking Age and Before*. Stockholm: Gidlunds Bokförlag.

Percy, Thomas. 1763. *Five Pieces of Runic Poetry Translated from the Islandic Language*. London: R. & J. Dodsley.

Roesdahl, Else. 1991. *The Vikings*, translated by Susan M. Margeson and Kirsten Williams. London: Allen Lane.

Wilson, David M., and Ole Klindt-Jensen. 1966. *Viking Art*. London: George Allen and Unwin Ltd.

Wolf, Kirsten. 2004. *Daily Life of the Vikings*. Westport, CT: Greenwood Press.

4

All Vikings Were Pagan

What People Think Happened

A common misconception is that all Vikings were pagan and worshipped gods like Odin, Thor, Frey, and Freyja. Additionally, many people know that Scandinavia converted to Christianity significantly later than the rest of Europe. The victims of the Viking raids who wrote about their sufferings undoubtedly had a hand in promoting the idea of Vikings as exclusively pagan and hostile toward Christians. The *Anglo-Saxon Chronicle*, for example, makes repeated mention of "heathen men" and a "heathen raiding-army" (Swanton 2000, 65, 67). To Christian Europe, tidings of brutal raids on monasteries by heathens were one of the worst things imaginable and left a lasting impression on the European perception of the Norse.

Another source contributing to the misconception of Vikings as exclusively pagan is Adam of Bremen's *Gesta Hammaburgensis ecclesiae pontificum* (*Activities of the Prelates of the Church of Hamburg*), written between 1073 and 1076. Adam was the director of the cathedral school in Bremen and had a vested interest in promoting the authority of the Hamburg-Bremen archbishopric over the newly Christianized regions of Scandinavia. Accordingly, it was advantageous for him to portray the Danes and Swedes in need of further Christianization, which was to be carried out through Bremen and bring those areas of Scandinavia into Germany's political sphere. Adam wrote that the German Emperor Otto II (955–983) pressured King Harald Bluetooth of Denmark (d. ca. 986) to convert to Christianity—an event conspicuously not supported by any other contemporary sources—in order to claim Denmark as a territory under the control of the German church (Winroth 2012, 113). Following the same motivation of advancing German authority, Adam continued to describe the famous heathen temple and sacrifices in Uppsala, Sweden. According to Adam, the temple housed statues of three gods. Thor, to whom one should appeal in the case of plagues and famines, stood in the center, flanked by Wodan (Odin) for war and Frikko (Frey) if weddings were to be celebrated. Adam also described a great ritual that took place at the temple every nine years and lasted for nine days, during which nine individuals of every male creature, including humans, were sacrificed and hanged in the nearby sacred grove. Such a vivid description of heathen sacrifices and Adam's mention of "unseemly incantations" would have done much to instill horror in devout Christians and offer a reminder of the heathen past that Scandinavians left behind much later than other Europeans.

How the Story Became Popular

Two works of Old Norse-Icelandic literature have shaped modern knowledge of Old Norse religion and, in turn, influenced perceptions of the Vikings more than any other sources. The first is a collection of Old Norse-Icelandic poetry on mythological topics known as the *Poetic Edda* preserved in the *Codex Regius* (the *King's Book*). The manuscript has been dated to around 1270, although some poems are considerably older (see chapter 3). The second is the so-called *Prose Edda*, written around 1220 by Snorri Sturluson (1178/9–1241), an Icelandic chieftain, historian, and poet. The book is a textbook to aid in the understanding and writing of skaldic poetry, a genre that relied on often-obscure references to specific mythological persons or events during a time when the details of the old heathen religion were fading from memory. These two works contain sketches of Norse cosmology; the names of gods, goddesses, giants, and dwarves; and myths about the beginning and the end of the world. These are the two extant sources that provide the most detail about ancient Germanic pre-Christian religion, and as a result, they became very influential.

In 1662, Bishop Brynjólfur Sveinsson (1605–1675) gave the *Codex Regius* to the king of Denmark (hence its name), where it became of interest to antiquarians and Scandinavian nationalists. The following century witnessed an increase of interest in Norse mythology outside of Scandinavia. Swiss writer Paul Henri Mallet translated the portion of Snorri's *Edda* that deals with the old gods and myths into French as *Monuments de la mythologie et de la poesie des Celtes, et particulierement des anciens*

Scandinaves (1756; *Monuments of the Mythology and the Poetry of the Celts, and Particularly the Ancient Scandinavians*), which was later translated into English by Thomas Percy in 1770 and revised by I. A. Blackwell in 1847 as *Northern Antiquities, Or, An Historical Account of the Manners, Customs, Religion and Laws, Maritime Expeditions and Discoveries, Language and Literature of the Ancient Scandinavians*. During the 19th century, Vikings and things Norse became a fashionable subject of study in Europe (see chapter 1). Thomas Hughes (1859) succinctly sums up the obsession with the pre-Christian religion and mythology of the north: "people sneer at the old English chronicles now-a-days, and prefer the Edda, and all sorts of heathen stuff" (37). Exotic images of Norse paganism went hand in hand with the romanticized image of the Viking. As a result, the reality of the more complex spectrum of religions in the Nordic region during the Viking Age was ignored in favor of wishful imaginings.

In 1825, Esaias Tegnér published his full poetic paraphrase translation of *Frithiofs saga*, which became hugely influential throughout the 19th century (see chapter 1). The many English translations by George Stevens (1839), Rowland Muckleston (1862), William Lewery Blackley (1867), Thomas A. E. and Martha A. Lyon Holcomb (1892), John B. Miller (1905), and Clement Burbank Shaw (1908) attest to the popularity of the poem well into the early 20th century. The plot centers on the Norwegian Frithiof, who falls in love with King Beli's daughter Ingeborg but is prevented from marrying her by the king's jealous successors and is sent to Orkney to collect tribute. When he returns, he finds his home burned down and Ingeborg married to the old King Ring. He burns down Baldr's temple and marries Ingeborg after King Ring dies. The poem is set before the days of Christianity, and the heathen gods and beliefs feature prominently, with frequent mentions of Odin, Thor, Frey, Baldr, Valhalla, runes, and Valkyries. Adam of Bremen's description of the statues of Thor, Odin, and Frey in the temple at Uppsala clearly served as a source: "[Frithiof] [m]ounted his father's seat, now his, and silently sat him / Down betwixt Odin and Frey; that is Thor's place up in Valhalla" (Blackley 1867, 30).

Many Viking novels followed in the wake of *Frithiofs saga*, all in the vein of the romanticized image of the heathen Viking. Several titles even include the name of Odin for additional exotic appeal: *Odin, A Poem* (1892), *The Hall of Odin* (1850), *Odin's Sagas* (1882), *Champion of Odin* (1885), and *Children of Odin* (1903) (Wawn 2000, 5). In the 20th century, the Viking moved to the silver screen, with *The Vikings* (1958), which was a very successful movie. The film creates a sharp contrast between the Vikings and the English. The former are depicted as wild, aggressive, impulsive, fur- and leather-dressed heathens, while the latter are portrayed as controlled, civilized, well-dressed Christians.

A popular portrayal of the Norse as pagans is the *Vikings* TV show, which first aired on March 3, 2013. The protagonists of the series are Ragnar Lothbrok (Travis Fimmel), Rollo (Clive Standen), Bjorn Lothbrok (Alexander Ludwig), Lagertha (Katheryn Winnick), and Queen Aslaug (Alyssa Sutherland), all pagan characters loosely based on historical or mythical characters. The show depicts violent conflicts among the Norse, Anglo-Saxons, and French, from a Scandinavian perspective. Some Christian viewers object to the representation of the heathen religion as more exciting and authentic than Christianity, which comes across as hypocritical, boring, and even depressing (West, 2016). However, in the 28th episode, "Breaking Point," Ragnar allows himself to be baptized in a manner similar to how many Norse were recorded to have done if it proved to be advantageous (Glader, 2016).

Finally, computer and video games have done more than their fair share to bolster the idea of Vikings as uniformly pagans. Some games with overt pagan Norse themes are "Valhalla" (1983), "Heimdall" (1992), "Ragnarok" (1992), "God of Thunder" (1993), "Viking: Battle for Asgard" (2008), "Jotun: Valhalla Edition" (2015), and "Vikings: Wolves of Midgard" (2017). The focus on heathen Vikings and the lack of representation of Christian Norse in books, films, and games during the 19th, 20th, and 21st centuries have perpetuated the misconception that all Viking Age Scandinavians were pagans.

PRIMARY DOCUMENT

ADAM OF BREMEN'S *ACTIVITIES OF THE PRELATES OF THE CHURCH OF HAMBURG* (11TH CENTURY)

This excerpt from Adam of Bremen's 11th-century Gesta Hammaburgensis ecclesiae pontificum *(Activities of the Prelates of the Church of Hamburg) describes the great pagan temple of Uppsala, Sweden, and the ritual sacrifice that took place there every nine years. He also describes a miracle that causes a former pagan priest to renounce his practices and believe in Christ, and the journey of Adalward, a missionary from Bremen, to destroy idols and convert some of the still-heathen Swedes.*

(25) . . . Now we shall say a few words about the superstitions of the Swedes.

(26) That folk has a very famous temple called Uppsala, situated not far from the city of Sigtuna and Björkö. In this temple, entirely decked out in gold, the people worship the statues of three gods in such wise that the mightiest of them, Thor, occupies a throne in the middle of the chamber; Wotan and Frikko have places on either side. The significance of these gods is as follows: Thor, they say, presides over the air, which governs the thunder and lightning, the winds and rains, fair weather and crops. The other, Wotan—that is, the Furious—carries on war and imparts to man strength against his enemies. The third is Frikko, who bestows peace and pleasure on mortals. His likeness, too, they fashion with an immense phallus. But Wotan they chisel armed, as our people are wont to represent Mars. Thor with his scepter apparently resembles Jove. The people also worship heroes made gods, whom they endow with immortality because of their remarkable exploits, as one reads in the *Vita* of Saint Ansgar they did in the case of King Eric.

(27) For all their gods there are appointed priests to offer sacrifices for the people. If plague and famine threaten, a libation is poured to the idol Thor; if was, to Wotan; if marriages are to be celebrated, to Frikko. It is customary also to solemnize in Uppsala, at nine-year intervals, a general feast of all the provinces of Sweden. From attendance at this festival no one is exempted. Kings and People all and singly send their gifts to Uppsala and, what is more distressing than any kind of punishment, those who have already adopted Christianity redeem themselves through these ceremonies. The sacrifice is of this nature: of every living thing that is male, they offer nine heads, with the blood of which it is customary to placate gods of this sort. The bodies they hang in the sacred grove that adjoins the temple. Now this grove is so sacred in the eyes of the heathen that each and every tree in it is believed divine because of the death or putrefaction of the victims. Even dogs and horses hang there with men. A Christian seventy-two years old told me that he had seen their bodies suspended promiscuously. Furthermore, the incantations customarily chanted in the ritual of a sacrifice of this kind are manifold and unseemly; therefore, it is better to keep silent about them.

(28) In that country there took place lately an event worth remembering and widely published because it was noteworthy, and it also came to the archbishop's attention. One of the priests who was wont to serve the demons at Uppsala became blind and the help of the gods was to no avail. But as the man wisely ascribed the calamity of blindness to his worship of idols, by which superstitious veneration he had evidently offended the almighty God of the Christians, behold, that very night a most beautiful

Virgin appeared to him and asked if he would put aside the images he had previously worshiped. Then he, who for the sake of this boon would refuse to undergo nothing that was hard, gladly promised he would. To this the Virgin answered: "Be completely assured that this place in which so much innocent blood is now shed is very soon to be dedicated to my honor. That there may not remain any trace of doubt in your mind about this matter, receive the light of your eyes in the name of Christ, who is my Son." As soon as the priest recovered his sight, he believed and, going to all the country about, easily persuaded the pagans of the faith so that they believed in Him who made the blind see.

(28) Impelled by these miracles, our metropolitan, forthwith obedient to the saying that runs, "Look up, and lift up . . . your eyes and see the countries; for they are white already to harvest," consecrated for those parts the younger Adalward, whom he took from the choir at Bremen, a man who shone in letters and for moral probity. Through legates of the most illustrious King Stenkhil he also fixed Adalward's see in the city of Sigtuna, which is a day's journey distant from Uppsala. But the way is such that, sailing the sea from Scania of the Danes, you will arrive at Sigtuna or Björkö on the fifth day, for they are close together. If, however, you go by land from Scania through the midst of the Gothic peoples and the cities Skara, Södertelge, and Björkö, it will take you a whole month to reach Sigtuna.

(29) Glowing with fervor, then, Adalward entered Sweden to preach the Gospel and in a short time led to the Christian faith all in Sigtuna and round about. He also secretly agreed with Egino, the most saintly bishop of Scania, that they should go together to the pagan temple called Uppsala to see if they could perhaps offer Christ some fruit of their labors there, for they would willingly undergo every kind of torture for the sake of destroying that house which was the seat of barbarous superstition. For, if it were torn down, or perfectly burned, the conversion of the whole nation might follow. Observing that the people murmured about this design of the confessors of God, the most pious king Stenkil shrewdly kept them from such an undertaking, declaring that they would at once be punished with death and he be driven from the kingdom for bringing malefactors into the country, and that everyone who now believed would quickly relapse into paganism, as they could see had lately been the case in Slavia. The bishops deferred to these arguments of the king and, going through all the cities of the Goths, they broke up idols and thereafter won many thousands of pagans to Christianity. When Adalward later died in our midst, the archbishop appointed in this place a certain Tadico of Ramesloh, who

out of love for his belly preferred even to starve at home rather than be an apostle abroad. Let these remarks about Sweden and its rites suffice.

Source: Adam of Bremen. 1959. *History of the Archbishops of Hamburg-Bremen,* translated by Francis J. Tschan. New York: Columbia University Press. 207–210. Reprinted with permission of Columbia University Press.

What Really Happened

The Christian/pagan divide in Scandinavia during the Viking Age was not all that clear-cut. Scandinavia is a large region, and the different areas did not convert to Christianity at the same time. Norwegian religious historian Fridtjov Birkeli (1973) divides the conversion process of Norway into the phases of infiltration (first contact and influence without conversion), mission (active attempts to convert individuals), and institution (adoption of the new religion by political leaders and imposed from above to the populace). This process can be applied to Denmark and Sweden as well. In the case of Scandinavia as a whole, infiltration began as early as 400, when Scandinavians came into contact with continental Germanic tribes and the Christian Roman Empire. The period of mission began in the ninth century, and the institution phase lasted from the early 11th century to the mid-12th century, when Christianity became established as the official religion in each of the Scandinavian countries.

Situated largely on the European continent, Denmark has always been closer to and more influenced by central European cultural currents, which similarly resulted in early contact with Christianity. In the first half of the ninth century, Ansgar (ca. 801–865), "the Apostle of the North," went on missions to Denmark and Sweden and succeeded in founding the first church in Scandinavia at Björkö, Sweden. After he had been appointed to the see of Bremen, which was united with Hamburg in 847/8, he also founded churches in Hedeby, Ribe, and Sigtuna. Nonetheless, Christianity did not become the official religion until around 965, when King Harald Bluetooth of Denmark (d. 986/87) converted to Christianity and raised what is likely the most famous runestone in existence, the inscription of which reads: "King Haraldr ordered [people] to make these monuments after Gormr, his father, and in memory of Thyrvé, his mother. That Haraldr who won for himself all of Denmark, and Norway, and made the Danes Christian" (Barnes 2012, 73).

In Norway, three kings had converted to Christianity and attempted to convert the country in the late 10th and early 11th centuries. Olaf Tryggvason (963–1000) and Olaf Haraldsson (995–1030) became Christians while raiding in the British Isles, and Hakon the Good (920–961), who had been raised in King Athelstan's (895–939) court, was baptized there (Holman 2003, 65). With the impetus of Christian rulers, who at times forcibly converted some of their subjects, Christianity gained ground. In 1152 or 1153, an archdiocese centered at Nidaros (modern-day Trondheim) was founded, which encompassed Norway and the settlements to the west.

The story of Iceland's conversion is related in detail in Ari Thorgilsson's *Íslendingabók* (the *Book of Icelanders*) written during the years 1118–1122. It tells that during the summer assembly in the year 1000, the heathen and Christian factions disagreed on which set of laws the country should adopt, and after deliberating for a day and a night, the pagan lawspeaker Thorgeir Thorkelsson decided that in order to maintain peace, only one set of laws should be applied to the country and so decreed that Iceland should become Christian. For several years, the old laws, which allowed infant exposure, eating horsemeat, and pagan sacrifice (as long as it was in secret), were maintained, but they were soon abolished (Brink 2012, 624–625).

Sweden was the last country to officially become Christian, though here too, there had been early practitioners of the new faith, largely as a result of Ansgar's missionary activity. However, there are few reliable sources about the status of Christianity in Sweden until the mid-12th century. The region was politically fragmented, and medieval sources describe relapses into paganism and struggles between heathenism and Christianity. Runestones testify to the growing acceptance of Christianity among the populace. Of the nearly 3,000 runestones in Sweden, more than 90 percent date from the period of conversion (Williams 1999, 62), and more than half exhibit a cross or a Christian prayer (Gräslund 2000, 270). Even pilgrimage to Christian destinations is mentioned on some runestones, such as the Uppland stone U 605, commissioned between roughly 1045 and 1075 by a woman named Ingirun for herself before her departure, in case she did not return from the perilous journey: "Ingirun, Hardr's daughter, had the runes carved in memory of herself. She wants to travel to the east and abroad to Jerusalem" (the Scandinavian Runic-Text Database). The old heathen religion continued in Uppland until sometime in the late 11th or early 12th century, and Sweden did not officially become integrated into the European church until 1164, when Uppsala became an archbishopric.

During the later Viking Age, there is evidence of religious syncretism, which is the blending of two religions. *Landnámabók* (the *Book of Settlements*) from the early 12th century describes the Icelandic settler Helgi, who appears to have been half-Christian and half-pagan: "Helgi's faith was very much mixed: he believed in Christ but invoked Thor when it came to voyages and difficult times" (Pálsson and Edwards 2006, 97). Another example of blended religion is a blacksmith's soapstone mold discovered in Denmark for forging pendants that could produce Thor's hammers and Christian crosses (Simek 1993, 219; for an illustration, see Wolf 2004, 165). Finally, it should be mentioned that some Vikings chose a form of preliminary or provisional baptism called *primo signatio* (prime signing), which allowed them to interact and trade with Christians, while still maintaining their heathen beliefs (Melnikova 2011, 104). A passage in *Egils saga Skalla-Grímssonar* (the *Saga of Egil Skalla-Grimsson*) describes how Egil and his brother Thorolf received this form of preliminary baptism from the English king Athelstan:

> The king asked Thorolf and Egil to take the sign of the cross, because that was a common custom then among both merchants and mercenaries who dealt with Christians. Anyone who had taken the sign of the cross could mix freely with both Christians and heathens, while keeping the faith that they pleased. Thorolf and Egil did so at the king's request, and both took the sign of the cross. (Scudder 1997, 84)

It may seem odd to think of Egil—a quintessential Viking in many ways and a feared warrior with an irascible temper and love for raiding—taking the sign of the cross, but his example supports the idea that the conversion process was gradual in Scandinavia. There had been Christians in Scandinavia since the early ninth century, but it seems that for several generations after the conversion, old habits and the new faith intermingled in often unexpected ways.

PRIMARY DOCUMENT
THE SAGA OF THE PEOPLE OF LAXARDAL (CA. 1250)

This excerpt from Laxdæla saga (*the* Saga of the People of Laxardal), *composed in Iceland around the middle of the 13th century, tells of a swimming contest between the Icelander Kjartan and the Norwegian king Olaf Tryggvason. After the contest, the king invites Kjartan and his men to stay with him in Trondheim for the winter, and introduces them to the Christian faith. At first Kjartan and his companions resist the king's offer, but eventually they change their minds and convert by their own free will.*

There were ten Icelanders altogether who went with Kjartan on this journey, and none would part with him for the sake of the love they bore him.

So with this following Kjartan went to the ship, and Kalf Asgeirson greeted them warmly. Kjartan and Bolli took a great many goods with them abroad. They now got ready to start, and when the wind blew they sailed out along Burgfirth with a light and good breeze, and then out to sea. They had a good journey, and got to Norway to the northwards and came into Thrandhome, and fell in with men there and asked for tidings. They were told that change of lords over the land had befallen, in that Earl Hakon had fallen and King Olaf Tryggvason had come in, and all Norway had fallen under his power. King Olaf was ordering a change of faith in Norway, and the people took to it most unequally. Kjartan and his companions took their craft up to Nidaross. At that time many Icelanders had come to Norway who were men of high degree. There lay beside the landing-stage three ships, all owned by Icelanders. One of the ships belonged to Brand the Bounteous, son of Vermund Thorgrimson. And another ship belonged to Hallfred the Trouble-Bard. The third ship belonged to two brothers, one named Bjarni, and the other Thorhall; they were sons of Broad-river-Skeggi, out of Fleetlithe in the east. All these men had wanted to go west to Iceland that summer, but the king had forbidden all these ships to sail because the Icelanders would not take the new faith that he was preaching. All the Icelanders greeted Kjartan warmly, but especially Brand, as they had known each other already before. The Icelanders now took counsel together and came to an agreement among themselves that they would refuse this faith that the king preached, and all the men previously named bound themselves together to do this. Kjartan and his companions brought their ship up to the landing-stage and unloaded it and disposed of their goods. King Olaf was then in the town. He heard of the coming of the ship, and that men of great account were on board. It happened one fair-weather day in the autumn that the men went out of the town to swim in the river Nid. Kjartan and his friends saw this. Then Kjartan said to his companions that they should also go and disport themselves that day. They did so. There was one man who was by much the best at this sport. Kjartan asked Bolli if he felt willing to try swimming against the townsman. Bolli answered, "I don't think I am a match for him." "I cannot think where your courage can now have got to," said Kjartan," so I shall go and try." Bolli replied, "That you may do if you like." Kjartan then plunges into the river and up to this man who was the best swimmer and drags him forthwith under and keeps him down for awhile, and then lets him go up again. And when they had been up for a long while, this man suddenly clutches Kjartan and drags him under; and they keep down for such a time as Kjartan thought quite long enough, when up they come a second time. Not a word had either to say to the other. The third time they went down together, and now they keep under for much the longest time, and Kjartan now misdoubted him how this play would end, and thought he had never before found himself in such a tight place; but at last they come up and strike out for the bank. Then said the townsman, "Who is this man?" Kjartan told him his name. The townsman said, "You are very deft at swimming. Are you as good at other deeds of prowess as at this?" Kjartan answered rather coldly, "It was said when I was in Iceland that the others kept pace with this one. But now this one is not worth much." The townsman replied, "It makes some odds with whom you have had to do. But why do you not ask me anything?" Kjartan replied, "I do not want to know your name." The townsman answered, "You are not only a stalwart man, but you bear yourself very proudly as well, but none the less you shall know my name, and with whom you have been having a swimming match. Here is Olaf the king, the son of Tryggvi." Kjartan answered nothing, but turned away forthwith without his cloak. He had on a kirtle of red scarlet. The king was then well-nigh dressed; he called to Kjartan and bade him not go away so soon. Kjartan turned back, but rather slowly. The king then took a very good cloak off his shoulders and gave it to Kjartan, saying he should not go back cloakless to his companions. Kjartan thanked the king for the gift, and went to his own men and showed them the cloak. His men were nowise pleased as this, for they thought Kjartan had got too much into the king's power; but matters went on quietly. The weather set in very hard that autumn, and there was a great deal of frost, the season being cold. The heathen men said it was not to be wondered at that the weather should be so bad; "it is all because of the new-fangled ways of the king and this new faith that the gods are angry." The Icelanders kept all together in the town during the winter, and Kjartan took mostly the lead among them. On the weather taking a turn for the better, many people came to the town at the summons of King Olaf. Many people had become Christians in Thrandhome, yet there were a great many more who withstood the king. One day the king had a meeting out at Eyrar, and preached the new faith to men—a long harangue and telling. The people of Thrandhome had a whole host of men, and in turn offered battle to the king. The king said they must know that he had had greater things to cope with than fighting there with churls out of Thrandhome. Then the good men lost heart and gave the whole case into the king's power, and many people were baptized then and there. After that, the meeting came to an end. That same evening the king sent men to the lodgings of the Icelanders, and bade them get sure knowledge of what they were saying. They did so. They heard much noise within. Then Kjartan began to speak, and said to Bolli, " How far are you willing, kinsman, to take this new faith the king preaches?" "I certainly am not willing thereto," said Bolli, "for their faith seems to me to be most feeble." Kjartan said, "Did ye not think the king was holding out threats against those who should be unwilling to submit to his will?" Bolli answered, "It certainly seemed to me that he spoke out very clearly that they would have to take exceeding hard treatment at his hands." "I will be forced under no one's thumb," said Kjartan, "while I have power to stand up and wield my weapons. I think it most unmanly, too, to be taken like a lamb in a fold or a fox in a trap. I think that is a better thing to choose, if a man must die in any case, to do first some such deed as shall be held aloft for a long time afterwards." Bolli said, " What will you do?" "I will not hide it from you," Kjartan replied; "I will burn the king in his hall." "There is nothing cowardly in that," said Bolli; "but this is not likely to come to pass, as far as I can see. The king, I take it, is one of great good luck and his guardian spirit mighty, and, besides, he has a faithful guard watching both day and night." Kjartan said that what most men failed in was daring, however valiant they might otherwise be. Bolli said it was not so certain who would have to be taunted for want of courage in the end. But here many men joined in, saying this was but an idle talk. Now when the king's spies had overheard this, they went away and told the king all that had been said. The next morning the king wished to hold a meeting, and summoned all the Icelanders to it, and when the meeting was opened the king stood up and thanked men for coming, all those who were his friends and had taken the new faith. Then he called to him for a parley the Icelanders. The king asked them if they would be baptized, but they gave little reply to that. The king said they were making for themselves the choice that would answer the worst. "But, by the way, who of you thought it the best thing to do to burn me in my hall?" Then Kjartan answered, "You no doubt think that he who did say it would not have the pluck to confess it; but here you can see him." "I can indeed see you," said the king, " man of no small counsels, but it is not fated for you to stand over my head, done to death by you; and you have done quite enough that you should be prevented making a vow to burn more kings in their houses yet, for the reason of being taught better things than you know and because I do not know whether your heart was in your speech, and that you have bravely acknowledged it, I will not take your life. It may also be that you follow the faith the better the more outspoken you are against it; and I can also see this, that on the day you let yourself be baptized of your own free will, several ships' crews will on that day also take the faith. And I think it likely to happen that your relations and friends will give much heed to what you speak to them when you return to Iceland. And it is in my mind that you, Kjartan, will have a better faith when you return from Norway than you had when you came hither. Go now in peace and safety wheresoever you like from the meeting. For the time being you shall not be tormented into Christianity, for God says that He wills that no one shall come to Him unwillingly." Good cheer was made at the king's speech, though mostly from the Christian men; but the heathen left it to Kjartan to answer as he liked. Kjartan said, "We thank you, king, that you grant safe peace unto us, and the way whereby you may most surely draw us to take the faith is, on the one hand, to forgive us great offences, and on the other to speak in this kindly manner on all matters, in spite of your this day having us and all our concerns in your power even as it pleases you. Now, as for myself, I shall receive the faith in Norway on that understanding alone that I shall give some little worship to Thor the next winter when I get back to Iceland." Then the king said and smiled, "It may be seen from the mien of Kjartan that he puts more trust in his own weapons and strength than in Thor and Odin." Then the meeting was broken up. After a while many men egged the king on to force Kjartan and his followers to receive the faith, and thought it unwise to have so many heathen men near about him. The king answered wrathfully, and said he thought there were many Christians who were not nearly so well-behaved as was Kjartan or his company either, "and for such one would have long to wait." The king caused many profitable things to be done that winter; he had a church built and the market-town greatly enlarged. This church was finished at Christmas. Then Kjartan said they should go so near the church that they might see the ceremonies of this faith the Christians followed; and many fell in, saying that would be right good pastime. Kjartan with his following and Bolli went to the church; in that train was also Hallfred and many other Icelanders. The king preached the faith before the people, and spoke both long and tellingly, and the Christians made good cheer at his speech. And when Kjartan and his company went back to their chambers, a great deal of talk arose as to how they had liked the looks of the king at this time, which Christians accounted of as the next greatest festival. "For the king said, so that we might hear, that this night was born the Lord, in whom we are now to believe, if we do as the king bids us." Kjartan says: "So greatly was I taken with the looks of the king when I saw him for the first time, that I knew at once that he was a man of the highest excellence, and that feeling has kept steadfast ever since, when I have seen him at folk-meetings, and that but by much the best, however, I liked the looks of him to-day; and I cannot help thinking that the turn of our concerns hangs altogether on our believing Him to be the true God in whom the king bids us to believe, and the king cannot by any means be more eager in wishing that I take this faith than I am to let myself be baptized. The only thing that puts off my going straightway to see the king now is that the day is far spent, and the king, I take it, is now at table; but that day will be delayed, on which we, companions, will let ourselves all be baptized." Bolli took to this kindly, and bade Kjartan alone look to their affairs. The king had heard of the talk between Kjartan and his people before the tables were cleared away, for he had his spies in every chamber of the heathens. The king was very glad at this, and said, "In Kjartan has come true the saw: 'High tides best for happy signs.' "And the first thing the next morning early, when the king went to church, Kjartan met him in the street with a great company of men. Kjartan greeted the king with great cheerfulness, and said he had a pressing errand with him. The king took his greeting well, and said he had had a thoroughly clear news as to what his errand must be, "and that matter will be easily settled by you." Kjartan begged they should not delay fetching the water, and said that a great deal would be needed. The king answered and smiled. "Yes, Kjartan," says he, "on this matter I do not think your eager-mindedness would part us, not even if you put the price higher still." After that Kjartan and Bolli were baptized and all their crew, and a multitude of other men as well. This was on the second day of Yule before Holy Service. After that the king invited Kjartan to his Yule feast with Bolli his kinsman. It is the tale of most men that Kjartan on the day he laid aside his white baptismal robes became a liegeman of the king's, he and Bolli both. Hallfied was not baptized that day, for he made it a point that the king himself should be his godfather, so the king put it off till the next day. Kjartan and Bolli stayed with Olaf the king the rest of the winter. The king held Kjartan before all other men for the sake of his race and manly prowess, and it is by all people said that Kjartan was so winsome that he had not a single enemy within the court. Every one said that there had never before come from Iceland such a man as Kjartan. Bolli was also one of the most stalwart of men, and was held in high esteem by all good men. The winter now passes away, and, as spring came on, men got ready for their journeys, each as he had a mind to.

Source: Press, Muriel A. C., trans. 1899. *Laxdæla Saga*. London: J. M. Dent. 131–141.

Further Reading

Barnes, Michael P. 2012. *Runes: A Handbook*. Woodbridge: Boydell.

Birkeli, Fridtjov. 1973. *Norske steinkors i tidlig middelalder; et bidrag til belysning av overgangen fra norrøn religion til kristendom*. Oslo: Universitetsforlaget.

Brink, Stefan. 2012. "Christianization and the Early Church." In *The Viking World*, edited by Stefan Brink and Neil Price. London: Routledge. 621–628.

Glader, Paul. 2016. "How the History Channel's 'Vikings' Series Shows a Dramatic Clash of Religion and Politics." *The Washington Post*, February 18. Accessed October 16, 2017. https://www.washingtonpost.com/news/acts-of-faith/wp/2016/02/18/how-the-history-channels-vikings-series-shows-a-dramatic-clash-of-religion-and-politics/?utm_term=.0ac514474305.

Gräslund, Anne-Sophie. 2000. "From Pagan to Christian—On the Conversion of Scandinavia." In *Vinland Revisited: The Norse World at the Turn of the First Millennium*, edited by Shannon Lewis-Simpson. St. John's: Historic Sites Association of Newfoundland and Labrador. 263–276.

Hughes, Thomas. 1859. *The Scouring of the White Horse*. Cambridge: Macmillan and Co.

Inscription code U 605. Recorded in Rundata 3.1 for Windows. Uppsala Universitet. Samnordisk runtextdatabas (Scandinavian Runic-text Database). Accessed October 15, 2017. http://www.nordiska.uu.se/forskn/samnord.htm/.

Melnikova, Elna. 2011. "How Christian Were the Vikings?" *Ruthenica* 4: 90–107.

Pálsson, Hermann, and Paul Edwards, trans. 2006. *The Book of Settlements: Landnamabok*. Winnipeg: University of Manitoba Press.

Scudder, Bernard, trans. 1997. "Egil's Saga." In *The Complete Sagas of Icelanders Including 49 Tales*, 5 vols., edited by Viðar Hreinsson. Volume 1. Reykjavík: Leifur Eiríksson. 46–139.

Simek, Rudolf. 1993. *A Dictionary of Northern Mythology*, translated by Angela Hall. Cambridge: D. S. Brewer.

Swanton, Michael, ed. and trans. 2000. *The Anglo-Saxon Chronicles*. London: Phoenix Press.

Tegnér, Esaias. 1867. *Frithiof's Saga*, translated by William Lewery Blackley. New York: Leypoldt & Holt.

West, Ed. 2016. "Vikings: How TV Drama Fell in Love with Bloodthirsty Paganism." *Catholic Herald*, May 27. Accessed October 14, 2017.

http://www.catholicherald.co.uk/commentandblogs/2016/05/27/vikings-how-tv-drama-fell-in-love-with-bloodthirsty-paganism/.

Williams, Henrik. 1999. "Runestones and the Conversion of Sweden." In *This Immense Panorama: Studies in Honour of Eric J. Sharpe*, edited by Carole M. Cusack and Peter Oldmeadow. Sydney: School of Studies in Religion, The University of Sydney. 59–78.

Winroth, Anders. 2012. *The Conversion of Scandinavia: Vikings, Merchants, and Missionaries in the Remaking of Northern Europe*. New Haven: Yale University Press.

Wolf, Kirsten. 2004. *Daily Life of the Vikings*. Westport, CT: Greenwood Press.

5

Vikings Were Hated by Their Peers

What People Think Happened

It is easy to imagine that the Vikings were hated everywhere because of the raids and destruction they wrought upon Europe. Contemporary authors from England, Ireland, and the European mainland portray them as mass murderers and complain bitterly about the devastation caused in their lands by the Vikings. In his letter home to King Aethelred of Northumbria from Charlemagne's court school in Aachen, Germany, soon after the unexpected and ferocious raid in 793 on the church and monastery on the tiny island of Lindisfarne just off the Northumbrian coast, the famous English priest and scholar Alcuin (d. 804) writes:

> Lo, it is nearly 350 years that we and our forefathers have inhabited this most lovely land, and never before has such terror appeared in Britain as we have now suffered from a pagan race, nor was it thought that such an inroad from the sea could be made. Behold, the church of St Cuthbert spattered with the blood of the priests of God, despoiled of all its ornaments; a place more venerable than all in Britain is given as a prey to pagan peoples. (Whitelock 1979, 776)

Ermentarius, a monk from Noirmoutier, France, writing in the 860s, gives the following account of the situation in the mid-ninth century on the western European mainland.

> The number of ships grows: the endless stream of Vikings never ceases to increase. Everywhere the Christians are victims of massacres, burnings,

plunderings. The Vikings conquer all in their path, and no one resists them. They seize Bordeaux, Périgueux, Limoges, Angouleme, and Toulouse. Angers, Tours, and Orléans are annihilated and an innumerable fleet sails up the Saine and the evil grows in the whole region. Rouen is laid waste, plundered, and burned, Paris, Beauvais and Meaux taken, Melun's strong fortress levelled to the ground, Chartres occupied and Evreux and Bayeux plundered, and every town besieged. (Graham-Campbell 1980, 31–32)

The anonymous author of *Cogadh Gaedhel re Gallaibh* (*The War between the Irish and the Foreigners*), written around 1114–1116, is even more descriptive in his account of the Irish people's intense hatred of the intruders:

In a word, although there were an hundred hard-steeled iron heads on one neck, and an hundred sharp, ready, never-rusting brazen tongues in every head, and an hundred garrulous, loud, unceasing voices from every tongue, they could not recount nor narrate nor enumerate nor tell what all the people of Ireland suffered in common, both men and women, laymen and priests, old and young, noble and ignoble, of hardship and injury and oppression in every house from these ruthless, wrathful, foreign, purely pagan people. (Magnusson 1980, 152)

In short, the Vikings had a very bad reputation.

How the Story Became Popular

The (mostly illiterate) Vikings themselves left little behind in terms of literature—save for some runic inscriptions that are short and formulaic—so eyewitness accounts of their atrocities come from their victims, several of whom were literate. The *Anglo-Saxon Chronicle*, for example, details the devastation caused by the Vikings in England, and the *Annals of St-Bertin* describes the attack on Dorestad, the main trading center of Frisia. Both the victims and the authors were, for the most part, Christians. As a result, several of the later perceptions of the Vikings have their origin in Christian propaganda, which focuses on the fact that the Vikings often targeted churches and monasteries. The Vikings did so for the simple reason that they could be sure that such sites contained treasures and were easy prey.

This one-sided picture of the Vikings as merciless barbarians, who were cast in the role of Antichrist by foreign writers, persisted for a long time. The Scandinavians and especially the Icelanders themselves did little to alter this picture of the Vikings in writings from the late Middle Ages, notably the Sagas of Icelanders, in their search for an impressive national identity, though in these works they were portrayed as national heroes. Moreover, past historians typically focused on the raids when writing about the Viking Age. The classic view of the Vikings is articulated especially in the 1958 movie *The Vikings*, which one critic described as a full-blooded depiction of rape and pillage. The revisionist attitude toward the Vikings did not begin until the 1960s or 1970s with the publications of Peter Sawyer's *The Age of the Vikings* (1962) and Peter Foote and David M. Wilson's *The Viking Achievement* (1970). Both are watershed publications in the sense that they focus less on the raids and more on the positive aspects of Scandinavian culture at the time and emphasize the Scandinavians' level of technological and organizational achievements.

A few modern writers, however, maintain that the bad reputation of the Vikings is justified. In his article in *The Independent* (April 5, 2014), British journalist Patrick Cockburn compares the atrocities of the Vikings to SS divisions invading Poland and claims that the intensity of their violence was equal to the civil war in Syria. His article concerns an exhibition entitled "Vikings: Life and Legend" in the British Museum in spring 2014. Cockburn takes exception to the view of most modern scholars, who emphasize that the Vikings comprised only a small portion of the population of Scandinavia, arguing that "the same could be said of the relationship between the SS and German society in its entirety." Skepticism about the modern, revisionist view of the Vikings is also voiced by Melanie McDonagh in an article in *The Spectator* (August 10, 2013), who wrote about the same exhibition, which at that time was in Copenhagen. Her assessment of the exhibition is that it "presents a different take on the Vikings than the revisionist notion of them as proto-feminists and early multiculturalists." She argues that "[i]n contrast to recent exhibitions which have focused on their (perfectly real) record as city founders, brilliant seafarers and traders with an interest in good governance, the exhibits return us to the traditional image of pillagers, raiders and aggressive colonisers: the artifacts are hard to square with them as peaceful farmers with an interest in travel". McDonagh draws attention to artifacts in the exhibition, such as swords, battle axes, lozenge-shaped arrows, and, not least, iron slave collars from Dublin. Based on an interview with David Dumville, a medievalist and Celtic scholar at the University of Aberdeen, she maintains that "the Vikings-as-peaceful-traders approach has now been academic orthodoxy for two generations" and laments that "its proponents are still getting grants as cutting-edge revisionists." She concludes her article by noting that "[t]he exhibition at the British Museum may be a good first step in what you might call the de-rehabilitation of the Vikings, without losing sight of the insights of the revisionists, chief of which is that they absolutely did not wear horned helmets."

PRIMARY DOCUMENT

C. F. KEARY, *THE VIKINGS IN WESTERN CHRISTENDOM* (1891)

The first extract is an example of one late 19th-century author's historical account of the Vikings. The chapter from which it is taken is called "Character of the Vikings," and the subsection is entitled "Love of Carnage." The author revels in the brutality of the Vikings and describes the weapons used in the raids. The second extract is the same author's description of the invasion of Germany.

The unbounded enthusiasm for battle and adventure which accompanied this life of treasure-seeking, which breathes in every line of the Eddic poetry, and which was in itself a kind of religion, is inexpressible by words. The Christian chroniclers give us the facts of the Viking raids—for this early period, they alone. But for the feelings which accompanied the adventurers we must turn to the native literature of the north, in which the old spirit fully survives. In these poems, and in them only, the scene of battle seems to take shape, and there is a wild magnificence in the picture that rises before our eyes.

We see the dragon ships with grinning heads cleaving their way through the water, churning it up with their tarred oars. If near the shadow of the land the boat is followed, perhaps, by a friendly troop of ravens, ready to make their account in the coming slaughter. This bird the Northmen have taken for the symbol of their 'war-wagers,' and use for their banner; and here and there a wise man among the crew, who has learnt the language of birds, hears the ravens (like the 'Twa Corbies' of the Scottish ballad) telling each other where the enemy are and where the thickest of the fight and the greatest slaughter will be. Or, maybe, far overhead rides a flock of wild swans, in which the eye of faith discerns the bright warlike shield-maidens of Odin—the spae-women, or Norns, as they are called sometimes—who weave the web of victory and defeat.

'The web is woven of the guts of men and weighed down with human heads. There are blood-stained darts to form the shafts; its stays are iron-wrought, with arrows shuttled. Strike with your swords this web of victory . . .

'Now the web is woven and the field reddened. Bloody clouds are gathering over the sky. The air shall be dyed with the blood of men. Let us ride away fast on our bare-backed steeds, with our drawn swords in our hands, far away.'

Then when the battle is joined. 'We hewed with swords. We reddened our swords far and wide. The moonlike shield was crimsoned [as the moon is when eclipsed], and shrilly screamed the swords. It was not like love-play when we were splitting of helms. Mighty was the onset. High rose the noise of the spears. . . . They rowed amain. They bent their backs to the oars. . . . The oar thongs split, the hawsers brake. . . . They hewed with their axes. . . . They put their fingers to the bowstrings and shot deftly. They covered themselves with their shields. So long as they remained alive they ceased not to hew with their swords, riving mail-coats and cleaving helmets. Through the morning they fought, through the first watches and till afternoon. The field was aswim with blood.'

Here is another passage in which, we may note, are mentioned nearly all the weapons in habitual use among the Northmen in the succeeding century, and probably also in use in this first Viking Age. 'The flying javelin bit; peace was belied there; the wolf was glad, and the bow was drawn; the bolts clattered; the spear-points bit; the flaxen bowstring bore the arrows out of the bow. He brandished the buckler on his arm, the rouser of the play of blades . . . The prince drew the yew, the wound-bees flew.'

The last is a curious and expressive synonym for the buzzing arrows.

Their shields hung round the bulwarks of the ship as it cleft the water—bright round shields, painted, say red or white, mainly of wood, with metal bosses, or covered with a plate of metal. In every way the Vikings were better armed than most of those against whom they fought; better armed for defence in their ring-sarks or byrnies; better for attack with their swords and axes; better armed than the peasant who took his place in the Saxon fyrd; far better than the members of the Irish hosting.

But in reading the accounts of battles in the Edda or Saga lays, we must remember that there was this difference between the later battles and those with which we are now concerned. It was during the second part of the Viking Age that naval battles became common. When they began they took place between rival members of the Scandinavian race, like a certain naval battle in Ireland which we shall describe hereafter. At the present time, and against the Christians, the Northmen could not fight such battles, simply because the Christians had no navies to oppose to them.

The ships as yet were vessels of transport, not of war. The men came out to fight on land. By the necessities of the case they were foot soldiers. This was no disadvantage to the Viking in England or in Ireland, where the opposing armies were likewise made up almost exclusively of foot soldiers. But on the Continent this arm of the service was all through the ninth century rapidly giving place to the horseman, who was the forerunner of the mediaeval knight. This change might and ought to have put the Northmen at a serious disadvantage, had the armies of the Lothairs and of Charles the Bald been more united or better handled. But the Vikings learnt from their enemies; and we read of them anon as so far taking a lesson from the Frank military system, that they began, when they landed, to seize horses from the peasantry in the neighbourhood and to ride over the country on them—a sort of mounted marines, as it were. When, in the latter half of our Viking Age, they had established regular colonies in France, they no doubt soon acquired all the military arts known to the Franks.

They had, we see, bows, spears, swords, and axes. Bows and arrows are very frequently mentioned in the Eddic songs, and we have many accounts of persons of note slain by the Viking arrows in the battles of this century. Swords and spears have furnished the most frequent remains in this kind, and are the most commonly mentioned in literature. The sword especially, though not originally characteristic of the Teutons, we may believe to have been among the Northmen a universal weapon. An armoury full of swords was the best kind of 'capital'; and sometimes one particular sword would be a disputed heirloom for generations. But perhaps the most distinctive and characteristic among Viking weapons (though this applies more especially to the Danes) was the axe. The Danes were as much celebrated for their axes as the Franks had been at an earlier date for theirs. But while the *francisca*, the axe of the Franks, had been a light weapon—of the tomahawk order almost, for it could be thrown as well as used for striking—the axes of the Danes were two-handed weapons of great weight and power, terrible in the hands of a compacted, well-disciplined host.

. . . .

The Vikings began by a widespread plundering over all the country of the Lower Rhine. After that they set out upon their march inland. Nobody was there to collect or take the command of an opposing army, and, the people fleeing out of their way as best they might, the Danes pressed on unhindered to Cologne, the metropolis of Lower Germany, almost the most important archbishopric north of the Alps. The greater part of the town the Vikings destroyed, and reduced its churches to ruins. Then forward to Bonn, which experienced the fate of Cologne. Zulpich, Julich, Neuss, fell at the same time. It might seem that this region which had witnessed the consolidation of the Frankish Empire was destined now to witness its entire overthrow. Worst of all they attacked and took imperial Aix itself. Now was fulfilled the threat of old Godfred the Danish king, against Charlemagne, that a Danish army should be seen within his capital; fulfilled by another Godfred, possibly his descendant. Old Godfred had never dreamt of such an easy victory as these Vikings were gaining, of so truculent an entry into the Capital of the Empire. The Northmen stalled their horses in the aisles of the churches which Charlemagne had built, and they plundered and in part burned the palace of the great emperor. From Aix the army passed on to the Abbey of Cornelimunster, and thence made their way into the beautiful Eifel country— that fair Devonian land—which was then no doubt very thinly inhabited. In the midst of that almost desert a bygone Carling prince had established the Abbey of Prum, which amid its matted brambles lay hidden from the world; yet not so hidden but that the Vikings could find it. It is a place much associated with the history of the Carling House. The great Charles had loved it and freely endowed it. Charles the Bald had been confined there when a boy, by the orders of his brother Lothair; and thither Lothair himself had gone to die when he laid down the imperial sceptre. It still awaited a third scion of the house to end his days in blind imprisonment within its walls; but at the moment he was watching, not altogether with discontent, the successes of the Danes.

The Vikings did not reach Prum until after the beginning of the new year, that is to say, on Twelfth Day, a.d. 882. This day was without question a heathen festival. At Prum they stayed three days, keeping we need not doubt high wassail. And this marked the farthest period of their advance in this expedition. For they now returned to a camp which they had made and fortified the year previous at Ashloh or Elsloo, a royal villa near Maestricht.

Terrible had been the doings of the heathen; and they were answered by signs not less terrible in earth and heaven. An earthquake shook men's very souls; in the January of this year a comet rose flaming into the night, and at the same time, the life ebbed away from Lewis of Germany, who had long been lying ill and incapacitated at Frankfurt.

Now Charles the emperor, once Charles of Swabia, was the inheritor of a vast domain. All the countries which, in former years, had been ruled by the three monarchs—Lewis the German, Lothair the Second, and Lewis the Emperor—were united under his sceptre. He did indeed promise to restore to his cousin the portion of Lorraine which had been ceded by the treaty of Ribemont; but he never fulfilled his promise. All these vast domains were nominally Charles's. But he was too weak to rule in them, or if he ruled to govern. In bad health, not unamiable, and beloved by many of his poorer subjects, he was yet not the man for these disjointed times.

Very soon the Northmen began again to advance up the Rhine. They were met by the joyful news of Lewis's death. Charles was in Italy, and Germany for the time without a ruler. Now was an opportunity for the Vikings to penetrate into the vine-lands which lay above the Mosel. The finest towns of Germany, the richest cathedrals and abbeys lay upon the stream up which their ships were sailing. If their leader Godfred really was—as some have supposed—the same as the Godfred, Harald's son, he might remember through the dim vista of years another occasion on which he had sailed in a white-winged Danish ship up the same reaches; passed Confluentes or Coblenz, where met the streams of Rhine and Mosel, past the Pfalzinsel where Lewis the Pious was carried to draw his last breath, through the narrow neck of river where the Lurlei rock mirrors itself in the swift stream, and up the broader reaches of the rich Rhinegau, as far as lordly Mainz. Now in a very different guise from that of humble, white-robed catechumens, and with fire and famine as their handmaids, he and his Danes set out upon the same journey. The people, sheep without shepherds, offered slight resistance. We have no details of this invasion. Those children of chaos, wherever they went, surrounded themselves with a cloud of darkness; for all that had any semblance of civilization fled at their approach. All the land between the Meuse and the Rhine, at any rate from Coblenz downwards, was in their hands, and it was passing more and more under the sceptre of Chaos and Old Night. And this was the region in which had been planted the germ of the mighty empire of the Franks. So far backwards had the Northmen contrived to roll the car of history. All of the Christians who could get there sheltered themselves within the walls of Mainz. Fortunately the invaders never got so far as this town. From Coblenz they turned up the Mosel and burnt Treves.

As the Danes were thinking of returning to their strong camp at Ashloh, the news reached them, and passed along all good Christian lips, that the new emperor, Charles, had come again across the Alps; that he had held a diet at Worms, and there had summoned contingents from every part of the empire. He was forming a great army, with which he was about to make a strenuous effort to rid Germany for ever from the Viking scourge.

And it was a huge army which now assembled under the banner of Charles. From Italy he had brought a body of Lombards, who were in this wise once again to revisit the neighbourhood of their own ancestral home, and once more to fight shoulder to shoulder with their ancient kinsmen, the Saxons. Contingents from all the German nationalities were with Charles's colours; his own Swabians; Bavarians under the leadership of Arnulf; East Franks under Duke Henry; Thuringians, Saxons, Frisians— who can count them all? A formidable host, had it been commanded by a man: if Arnulf, for example, instead of being second in command, could have been first.

Source: Keary, C. F. 1891. *The Vikings in Western Christendom A.D. 789 to A.D. 888.* New York: C. P Putnam's Sons. 168–172, 452–456.

What Really Happened

Yes, the Vikings were hated by many people. And yes, they were brutal, but maybe not more brutal than other people at the time. Anders Winroth (2014, 42) draws attention to the fact that in 782, Charlemagne had no fewer than 4,500 Saxons decapitated in a single day and points out that the only difference between Charlemagne's mass murder and the execution of many people by the Vikings is that there are no preserved eyewitness accounts of Charlemagne's slaughter.

However, some people(s) appreciated and respected the Vikings and took advantage of their skills. One example of a Viking who ended up serving in the interest of an area targeted by Viking raids is the late ninth-century's Hrolf (better known perhaps as Rollo), known primarily from *Göngu-Hrólfs saga* (the *Saga of Ganger-Hrolf*), a mythical heroic saga from the early 14th century, and the biography of him written by Dudo of Saint-Quentin, a monk from Vermondois, who compiled a history of the first Norman dukes (*De moribus et actis primorum normanniae ducum*) in the early 11th century. According to the Old Norse-Icelandic saga, Hrolf was the son of a Norwegian earl and spent his early years as a Viking, pillaging in the Baltic. He then took off to the Hebrides, where he joined other Vikings, who raided on both sides of the English Channel. Little is known about Hrolf's/Rollo's activities until 911, although it is quite possible that he was a member of the so-called great heathen army, which attacked England from the continent. What is known about him is that he was the leader of the army that laid siege to Chartres, France. On this particular occasion, the Vikings were defeated, but the king, Charles III the Simple (879–929), cleverly saw this as an opportunity to enlist the Vikings as watchdogs against further attacks by Vikings. So he shrewdly offered the Viking invaders the land they already occupied. In return, the Vikings swore to Charles III an oath of allegiance, and Rollo was made the duke of Normandy. In this way, the Viking colony of Normany (or Nothmannia, the land of the northmen) came into existence, and Rollo's dynasty ruled the province in direct line until 1204, when King Philip Augustus (1165–1223) annexed the duchy to the royal domain and abolished the office of the duke (Magnusson 1980, 281–284).

Another example of a well-liked Viking is the Dane Rørik (better known, perhaps, as Roric or Roricus), whose uncle had been king of Denmark. Like Rollo, he spent the earlier part of his life as a Viking, plundering the kingdom of Emperor Lothar (795–855) and did so using the kingdom of Lothar's enemy brother, Louis the German (ca. 804–876), as his base. Roric attacked and besieged the town of Dorestad, a major trading center, in 850, and when it became apparent to Emperor Lothar that he could not suppress Roric and his army, he appointed him as his vassal in order to ward off further Viking attacks. After the death of Emperor Lothar, Roric sought out Louis the German and pledged allegiance to him as well, though Roric remained in Dorestad and became, in essence, the vassal of both Louis the German and Emperor Lothar's successor. His rule covered most of what is now currently the Netherlands.

Finally, mention should be made of the Varangian Guard, an elite unit of the Byzantine army from the 10th to the 14th centuries. The members of the unit—somewhat comparable to the Navy SEALs today—were highly trained warriors. Upon swearing an oath to the Byzantine emperor, they served as his bodyguard and were deployed at critical moments of a battle. Their duties correspond in many ways to the Norwegian *hird* or the Anglo-Saxon housecarls, both terms for the retinue of warriors accompanying a king or a warlord. For the first century or so, the earliest members were the Rus, Scandinavians living in what is now Ukraine and Belarus. During the second century of the organization, men from Scandinavia, primarily Sweden, joined, and after the Norman conquest of England, there was a significant increase of Anglo-Saxon members. Several Swedish runestones were raised in memory of men who died in Greece, possibly as members of the Varangian Guard. Examples include U 112: "Ragnvaldr had the runes carved in memory of Fastve, his mother, Onæmr's daughter, [who] died in Eid. May God help her spirit. Ragnvaldr had the runes carved; [he] was in Greece, was commander of the retinue" (Scandinavian Runic-text Database) and U 792: "Karr had this stone raised in memory of Haursi(?), his father; and Kabbi/Kampi/Kappi/Gapi(?)

in memory of his kinsman-by-marriage. [He] travelled competently; earned wealth abroad in Greece for his heir" (Scandinavian Runic-text Database). In addition, there are runic inscriptions in the mosque of Hagia Sophia in Constantinople (now Istanbul) carved by a Scandinavian, who likely served as a member of the Guard (see chapter 1), and on a marble statue of a lion, which stood in Piraeus, the port city for Athens in the Viking Age. (For illustrations, see Magnus Magnusson 1980, 119 and 27.)

No doubt, the most famous Scandinavian to enter the service was Harald Hard-Ruler Sigurdsson, king of Norway 1046–1066. His career is narrated primarily in Snorri Sturluson's (1178/9–1241) *Heimskringla* (*Disc of the World*), which provides an account of his years as a leader of the Varangian Guard. A Greek work, *Logos nuthetikos*, from the late 11th century also mentions his campaigns.

The men on the islands newly settled by Scandinavians in the Atlantic seem to have entered the service somewhat later, but the composers of the Sagas of Icelanders were clearly very proud of any young Icelander who served as a member of the Guard and speak or write of them in glorious terms. It is known from *Laxdæla saga* (the *Saga of the People of Laxardal*) from around the middle of the 13th century that Bolli Bollason (b. ca. 1006) was a member of the Varangian Guard. The saga reports that after traveling via Norway, Denmark, and other countries, Bolli arrived at Constantinople, where he entered the company of the Varangian Guard. The composer of the saga claims that "we know of no reports of northerners having entered the service of the Byzantine emperor" and adds that Bolli "spent many years in Constantinople, where he was regarded as the most valiant of fighters in any perilous situation, where he was among the foremost of men. The Varangians thought highly of Bolli during his stay in Constantinople" (Kunz 2007, 112). Evidently, Bolli did well. The composer of the saga describes his return from Byzantium as follows:

> Four winters after the drowning of Thorkel Eyjolfsson a ship owned by Bolli Bollason sailed into Eyjafjord. Most of the crew were Norwegians. Bolli had brought with him a great deal of wealth from abroad and many treasures given him by princes. He had become such a fine dresser by the time he returned from his journey abroad that he wore only clothes of scarlet or silk brocade and all his weapons were decorated with gold. He became known as Bolli the Elegant . . . He wore a suit of silk brocade given to him by the emperor of Byzantium, with a cloak of red scarlet outermost . . . He had a lance in his hand, as is common in foreign parts. Wherever the group stopped for the night, the women could do nothing but gaze at Bolli and the finery which he and his companions wore. (Kunz 2007, 118)

There are further references in the Sagas of Icelanders to Icelanders serving in the Varangian Guard. Examples include *Njáls saga* (the *Saga of Njal*), *Hrafnkels saga* (the *Saga of Hrafnkel*), and *Grettis saga* (the *Saga of Grettir*).

PRIMARY DOCUMENT
THE SAGA OF HARALD HARD-RULER (CA. 1230)

The extract is from Haralds saga harðráða (*the* Saga of Harald Hard-Ruler) *in Snorri Sturluson's* Heimskringla. *It tells that Harald spent 15 years in the service of the Kievan prince Jaroslav, whose daughter he married, and in the imperial service in Byzantium.*

It befell in the days of the fall of King Olaf that Harald, the son of Sigurd Sow, the stepbrother of King Olaf the Saint, bore his share in the great battle of Stiklastad. Even there it befell Harald that he was smote down, but he gained the life of his body by flight with others that bore him company. Thus saith Thiodolf:

'Nigh the hill, a battle-storm
I heard drive toward the King,
But the burner of the Bulgars
His brother well supported.
Unwillingly from fallen Olaf
Was the prince sundered,
And his head he hid;
Then was he twelve winters
With added three thereto in age.'

It was Rognvald Brusason who bare Harald out of the battle, and brought him to a certain peasant who lived in the forest, and that in a glade far from the haunts of man; and here was Harald leeched until he was whole of his wound. Thereafter fared forth the son of that peasant eastward with him across the Kjol (Kiolen), & as far as they were able to do so followed they forest tracks in lieu of the common way. Now in no wise wist the son of the peasant with what manner of man he was faring, & as they were riding through the wastes of the forest sang Harald thus wise:

'From forest now to forest
Wend I my way with honour scant;

Who wists but in the future
Wide fame may not be mine?'

And thus fared he eastward through Jamtaland & Helsingland, and in due course was he come even to Sweden; there did he link his fortune with that of Rognvald Brusason and many others of the men of King Olaf that were yet alive after the mighty battle.

Now in the spring thereafter gat they ships for themselves and in the summer fared eastward to Garda, where abode they the winter through with King Jarizleif. Thus saith Bolverk:

'The sword's blade, King, thou dried'st
When thou fared'st from the strife.
To the raven gav'st thou to eat;
The wolf howled on the wooded heights.
But the year thereafter and thou wert
East in Gard, O doughty fighter,
Ne'er have I heard of a leader of hosts
More famed than thou wert.'

King Jarizleif made Harald & his men welcome right kindly, and even so became Harald captain of the land defence of the King & with him was joined Eilif, the son of Earl Rognvald. Thus saith Thiodolf:

'Where Eilif was,
Alike they acted,
Those chieftains twain
In wedge-like phalanx.
Chased were the East Wends
Into a corner narrow,
Not easy for the Laesirs
Was the law of the host.'

Some winters abode Harald in the realm of Garda, & fared forth for the most part eastward; then went he a journey to Greece, and in his company was a mighty following, and at that time likewise went he to Miklagard (Constantinople). Saith Bolverk:

'The chilly shower drave forward
The ship's swart prows;

And barks all bravely armoured
Their sails bore by the coast-side.
The metal towers of Miklagard
128 The prince saw from the prows;
Fair-bosomed ships were borne
To the walls of the city.'

At that time there ruled over Greece Queen Zoe the Wealthy and with her Michael Katalaktus. When Harald was come even unto Miklagard in the hardiness that was of his blood enterprised he service of the Queen, and even so did the men that were with him. Forthwith that same autumn took he ship on certain galleys with warriors who were adventuring on to the Greek sea. In those days was one named Gyrgir chief of the hosts, and he was also a kinsman to the Queen. Now it came to pass that Harald had not abode longtime with the host ere the Vaerings became much drawn to him, so that he and they adventured all together in a body whensoever there was fighting, and the end thereof was that Harald was chosen captain of all the Vaerings. Gyrgir and his hosts coasted in all directions among the Greek islands, and greatly plundered the corsairs.

Once it befell when they were faring overland, and were of a mind to pass the night in the woods, that the Vaerings were the first to come to the place where it was intended they should lie, and chose they for their tents even such position as was best and lay highest, for the country thereabout was boggy, and no sooner came the rain than was it ill living there over against where the land was low. Then came Gyrgir, & when he saw where the Vaerings had pitched their tents bade he them begone and pitch them in another place, since saith he, that he himself would have his tent even there. But thus spake Harald: 'When ye are the first to come to the place for the camp then shall ye make choice of your place for the night, and it will behove us to pitch our tents elsewhere, even in whatever spot is open to us. So do ye now likewise; pitch ye your tents where ye will in any other spot that pertaineth. Methought was it the right of the Vaerings here in Greece to be masters of their own matter & free in all things before all men, and that was it to the King and Queen only they owed obedience.' On this bandied they words with so great heat that both sides fell to arming themselves, & right nigh came they to fighting, but ere that were the wisest men came up and they parted them. They said it was more in reason that these men should be of one mind on the matter, and a just decision made thereon betwixt them, so that never more might strife arise out of this cause. So then was agreed a meeting between them, & the best and wisest men were present thereat; and at that meeting was it counselled in such manner that all were of one mind, to wit, that lots should be borne in a cloth and cast between Greek and Vaering as to who should be the first to ride or row, or berth them in haven, or choose a spot for their tents; both of them henceforth to rest content with whatever the lot decreed. Thereafter was this done, and the lots were marked; then said Harald to Gyrgir; 'Let me now see how thou markest thy lot, to the intent that we may not both mark them in the same fashion.' So Harald looked and thereafter marked his lot and threw it into the cloth, and Gyrgir did likewise; but the man who was to draw the lot took up one between his fingers, and lifting his hand said: 'These shall first ride and row and berth them in haven and choose them tent-places.' Then did Harald seize the lot with his hand and throw it out into the sea, and when he had so done he said: 'That was our lot.' Gyrgir said: 'Why didst thou not let more men see it?' 'Look you,' answered Harald, 'on that lot which is left, & I wot well thereon will you know your own mark.' Then looked they at the lot, and all knew the mark to be that of Gyrgir. So was it adjudged that the Vaerings should have the choice in all those matters about which there had been strife. Sundry things befell likewise on which saw they not eye to eye, but ever it ended in such a fashion that Harald had his way.

Plundering & pillaging whithersoever they went fared together both hosts during the summer, but when a battle was imminent would Harald cause his men to hold aloof therefrom, or at least over against that part where was the fight most open. Ever said he that he would take good care that he did not lose those that were of his company; but when a fight chanced and he with his men only were opposed to an enemy so fierce was he in battle that either must he win the day or die. For this reason oft-times it befell that when Harald was captain of the men the victory fell to him, whereas Gyrgir won naught. Now when the warriors saw how oft did this come to pass, said they one to the other that their cause would have better advancement an Harald were alone captain of the host; and blamed they the leader of the band, saying that he and his men were but bootless. To this Gyrgir made answer that the Vaerings would not yield him support, & bade them begone, whiles he fared with the rest of the host to be successful as far as in them lay. Even so, thereon went Harald from the host, and with him likewise the Vaerings and the Latin men, but Gyrgir kept the host of the Greeks. Then came to pass that which all had awaited, to wit, that Harald ever gained the victory & the plunder. Thereupon fared the Greeks home to Miklagard save only the young men who desired to win riches for themselves, and they gathered round Harald and took him for their leader. Then went he with his host westward to northern Africa, which the Vaerings called Serkland, and there he gained addition to his host. In Serkland won he eighty walled towns, some thereof surrendered to him, whereas others took he by might. Thereafter went he to Sikiley (Sicily). Thus saith Thiodolf:

'Towns ten times eight in Serkland,
Say I, then were taken,
The young hater of red-glowing gold
Rushed into the peril.
Before the fighter went to rouse
With clashing shields the Hilds,
Were they long the Serk-men's foe,
On the plains of Sicily.'
Thus saith Illugi, the skald from Bryn:
'Harald under Michael strove
For south-lands with his sword
The son of Budli, as 'twas said
Showed friendship by his fellowship.'

Now it came to pass that at this season was Michael King of Greece. Many winters abode he in Africa, and to himself acquired goods and chattels in plenty, gold likewise and all manner of precious things; but all the wealth which he took and thereof had not need for his maintenance sent he by his trusty men to Holmgard (Novgorod), to be bestowed into the hands and care of King Jarizleif. Exceeding wealth did he collect together there, as was like to be, forasmuch as he was pillaging in that part of the world the which is richest in gold and costly things. And so much did he accomplish withal that, as has been writ before, took he as many as eighty towns.

And being come to Sikiley did Harald lay waste on that isle, and set he his host over against a large town in which were many people. So strong were the walls thereof that he feared it were doubtful an he could brake them down. Now the townsfolk had enough of victuals and other commodities which were required to withstand a siege, so hit Harald on the craft of bidding his fowlers to catch small birds, which had nests in the town & flew out during the day to seek food. On the backs of these birds caused he to be tied shavings of red pine-wood on which had he poured melted wax and brimstone; fire thereto was set, and the birds even so soon as they were loose, flew with one accord at once to the town with the intent to seek their young and to hie them to their own nests which were under the roofs. And these roofs were thatched with reeds or straw. Then the fire from the birds spread to the eaves, and though each bird bore but a little burden of fire nevertheless in a brief space was kindled a great fire, for many birds bore fire to the roofs that were of the town. Thereafter there burned one house after the other until the town itself was all aflame, and all the people came out therefrom and begged for grace. Yea was this that same folk that for many a day had talked proudly and with mocking despite of the Greek host and the chief thereof. Harald gave quarter to all men who craved it, and thereafter held authority over this town.

Another town was there to which Harald went with his host, & right well peopled was it and strong withal, so much so indeed that it could not be thought that he would be able to make assault thereon. Flat land and hard lay round about the walls thereof, so Harald set his men to dig a trench from the place whence a brook flowed, & that in a deep gulley wherein men from the town could not spy. The earth of the trench threw they out into the water and let the stream bear it away; and in this work they continued even both by night and by day with fresh shifts after a spell. After this fashion did the host advance on the town day by day; and the townsmen flocked to the battlements & both sides shot at one another, but by night did all betake themselves to sleep. Now when Harald wot that this hole that was in the earth was so long that it must have come under and past the walls of the town bade he his men arm themselves, & towards dawn went they into the trench, and when they came to the end thereof dug they up above their heads until they came to stones set in lime; and this was the floor of a stone hall. Anon they brake up the floor and ascended into the hall, and there sat many of the townsmen eating and drinking, and great was the mischance of these good men for they were taken unawares. The Vaerings went about with drawn swords, and straightway killed some of them though others fled, to wit, those who could get out. Some of the Vaerings sought after these townsmen while others went to the gates to set them open, and by this way in marched the host that pertained unto Harald. Then did the townsfolk flee, though many prayed for mercy, and mercy did all receive who gave themselves up. In this way was it that Harald was possessed of the town, and therewith acquired exceeding wealth.

The third town to which they came was the one that of all of the island had waxed largest and strongest, and to it pertained most importance both by reason of the wealth and the number within its walls. Even about this town lay great ditches, and the Vaerings marked that they could not win it by craft after such fashion as they had possessed themselves of the other towns aforesaid. And so it came to pass that long lay they before the town yet did they accomplish nothing, and the townsfolk seeing this waxed even bolder, and set up their array on the walls, & anon opened the gates of the town and called to the Vaerings, egging them on & bidding them enter; and they mocked at them for lack of boldness, averring that for fighting were they no better than so many hens. Harald bade his men behave themselves as though they wist not after what fashion were such things said: 'Nought shall we accomplish,' said he, 'even if we storm the town; they will fling their weapons down under their feet upon us; and albeit an entrance we perchance effect with sundry of our folk, yet is the foe strong enough to shut them in, and shut the others out at their pleasure for they have put watches at all the gates of the town. No less mock will we make of them, however, and we will flaunt in their faces that we have no fear of them. Our men shall go forth on the plain as near the town as may be, having care nevertheless lest they come within bowshot, and weaponless must they go & hold sports one with another so that the townsfolk may wot that we care naught for their array.' After this fashion did they behave themselves for sundry days.

Now of the Icelanders that were with Harald at this time is it recorded that Halldor the son of Snorri the Priest—he it was who took this chronicle back to his own land—and in the second place Ulf the son of Uspak, the son of Usvif the Wise, were the twain of them very strong & valiant men and much cherished of Harald. The pair were alike foremost in the sports on the plain. When things had thus happened for these sundry days, were the townsfolk minded to show even greater arrogance, & discarding their weapons mounted they up on to the walls and defiantly set open the gates of the town. Now the Vaerings seeing this betook themselves one day to their sports in such fashion that the swords that pertained to them were concealed beneath their cloaks and their helms beneath their hats. And after they had vied with one another awhile saw they that the townsfolk in no fashion entertained suspicion, thereon drawing their swords ran they forward to the gates. When the townsmen saw this advanced they bravely to meet them, standing fully armed, and thereon ensued a dire fight within the gates. To the Vaering folk pertained neither shield nor buckler, & in default thereof wrapped they their cloaks round their left arm; some were wounded, some killed, & all were hard pressed. Harald & the men with him who were in the camp hastened to their succour, but by then were the townsfolk come up on to the walls from whence they shot at & stoned those coming thitherwards. Yet more fierce grew the fight, & those within the gates bethought them help came at a slower gait than they could desire. Scarce was Harald come to the gates ere was slain his banner-bearer; then said he: 'Halldor, do thou take up the banner!' Halldor picked up the banner-staff, but he spoke unwisely: 'Who will bear thy banner for thee when thou followest it so faint-heartedly as thou hast done now this while past?' These were words more of anger than of truth, for Harald stood the stoutest among men. Then hied they them into the gate, and great were the strokes given; but the outcome thereof was such wise that the victory was to Harald and he stormed the gates. Sore smote was Halldor, a deep wound gat he in the countenance, and to him was it a blemish all the days of his life.

The fourth town whereunto Harald was come together with his host was the stoutest of all those whereof we have yet told. So strong was it that they wist there was no hope that it could be taken by assault, and thereon beset they the town even by getting a ring around it so that no victuals could be taken therein. Now it chanced when Harald had been before it a while, fell he sick and betook himself to his bed; & he caused his tent be placed away from other tents so that he might have the ease that he should not hear the noise and disquiet of the host. Backwards & forwards to him oft fared his men, craving his counsel, and this was noted of the townsfolk who argued rightly that something had befallen the Vaerings, and thereon set they spies to discover what it might be. When the spies were come back even into the town brought they intelligence that the chief of the Vaerings lay sick, & for that cause had they not advanced on the town. As time waxed big grew the strength of Harald small, and his men became sorrowful and were heavy of heart. Now of all this had the townsfolk full knowledge. To such a pass came it that the sickness pressed Harald hard and his death was told throughout the whole host. Then went the Vaerings to speak with the townsmen, telling them of the death of their chief, & praying the priests to grant him a tomb in the town. Now when the townsfolk heard these tidings many were there, rulers of monasteries or of other big churches in the town, who wished much, each one of them, to have the body for his church, for well wotted each that it would bring them great offerings; so the whole multitude of the priests clad themselves in their vestments and walked forth out of the town in procession well favoured and solemn, bearing shrines and holy relics. But made the Vaerings also a mighty funeral train; covered with a costly pall was the coffin borne aloft, and above this again were held many banners, & after the coffin in this wise had been borne in through the town-gates was it set down right athwart them in front of the opening thereof. Then did the Vaerings blow a war-blast from all their trumpets, & drew their swords, and the whole host of the Vaerings rushed out of their tents fully armed, and ran towards the town shouting and crying. The monks & other priests who had been walking in this funeral train vying with one another to be the foremost to go out and receive the offering, now vied twofold as speedily to be the farthest off, for the Vaerings slew every one who was nearest to them be he clerk or layman. After this fashion did they go about the whole of the town, putting the men to the sword and pillaging the churches, whence snatched they exceeding great wealth.

Many summers fared Harald in warfare after this fashion alike in Serkland and Sikiley. Thereafter led he his host back to Miklagard, and abode there a short space ere set he again forth on a journey to Jorsalaheim (Palestine). There he left behind him all the gold he had gotten as payment from the Greek King, & the same did all the Vaerings who went on the journey with him. It is told that altogether Harald fought eighteen battles on these journeys. Thus saith Thiodolf:

'All men know that Harald
Eighteen battles grim hath fought,
Oft hath the peace of the chieftain been broken;
The gray eagle's sharp claws
In blood didst thou dye, King,
Ever was the wolf filled ere thou fared'st homeward.'

Harald with his men had now betaken themselves to Jorsalaland (Palestine) and thence to Jorsalaborg (Jerusalem), and whithersoever he went in Jorsalaland were all the towns and castles surrendered unto him; thus saith Stuf, who had himself heard the King recount these things:

'The blade-bold smiting warrior
To subjection brought Jerusalem.
The smiling land was captive to him and the Greeks,
And by their might, unburned withal,
Came the country under the warrior's dictate.'

Here it is recounted that this land came unburned and unscathed into Harald's power. Thereafter fared he to the Jordan and bathed himself therein, as is the way with other pilgrims. On the Sepulchre of the Lord, the Holy Cross, and other holy relics in Jorsalaland bestowed Harald great benefactions. Then did he make safe all the road to the Jordan, slaying robbers and other disturbers of the peace. Thus saith Stuf:

'By counsel and wrathful words the King of the Agdir folk
Withstood on the banks of the Jordan the treason of men,
But for true trespass had folk to pay dearly;
Ill from the Prince suffered they.
(In Christ's eternal house).'

After these things fared he back to Miklagard.

> **Source:** Hearn, Ethel H., trans. 1911. *The Sagas of Olaf Tryggavson and of Harald the Tyrant*. London: Williams and Norgate. 127–137.

Further Reading

Cockburn, Patrick. 2014. "The Vikings Were Feared for a Reason." *The Independent*, April 5. Accessed October 14, 2017. http://www.independent.co.uk/voices/comment/the-vikings-were-feared-for-a-reason-9241032.html.

Foote, Peter, and David M. Wilson. 1970. *The Viking Achievement: The Society and Culture of Early Medieval Scandinavia*. London: Sidgwick & Jackson.

Graham-Campbell, James. 1980. *The Viking World*. New Haven: Ticknor and Fields.

Inscription code U 112. Recorded in Rundata 3.1 for Windows. Uppsala Universitet. Samnordisk runtextdatabas (Scandinavian Runic-text Database). Accessed October 15, 2017. http://www.nordiska.uu.se/forskn/samnord.htm/.

Inscription code U 792. Recorded in Rundata 3.1 for Windows. Uppsala Universitet. Samnordisk runtextdatabas (Scandinavian Runic-text Database). Accessed October 15, 2017. http://www.nordiska.uu.se/forskn/samnord.htm/.

Jefferies, Henry A. 1993. "Cogadh Gaedhel re Gallaibh." In *Medieval Scandinavia: An Encyclopedia*, edited by Phillip Pulsiano and Kirsten Wolf. New York: Garland Press.

Kunz, Keneva, trans. 2007. "The Saga of the People of Laxardal." In *The Complete Sagas of Icelanders Including 49 Tales*, edited by Viðar Hreinsson. Volume 5. Reykjavík: Leifur Eiríksson Publishing. 1–120.

Magnusson, Magnus. 1980. *Vikings!* New York: E. P. Dutton.

McDonagh, Melanie. 2013. "Sorry—The Vikings Really Were That Bad." *The Spectator*, August 10. Accessed October 15, 2017. https://www.spectator.co.uk/2013/08/sorry-the-vikings-really-were-that-bad/.

Sawyer, Peter. 1962. *The Age of the Vikings*. London: Arnold.

Whitelock, Dorothy, ed. 1979. *English Historical Documents, c. 500–1042*. Rev. ed. English Historical Documents. Volume 1. London: Eyre & Spottiswoode.

Winroth, Anders. 2014. *The Age of the Vikings*. Princeton: Princeton University Press.

6

Wives of Vikings Had Equal Rights

What People Think Happened

When on April 8, 1999, first lady Hillary Rodham Clinton gave a speech at the opening of an exhibit featuring the Vikings in the National Museum of Natural History in Washington, DC, she mentioned that she'd been interested to learn that "within Viking society, women had a good deal of freedom—to engage in trade and to become active participants in the political lives of their communities." With her statement, Mrs. Clinton perpetuated what seems to be a common misconception about the freedom and high status of women in Viking Age Scandinavia. Although it is possible that women in Viking Age Scandinavia enjoyed more respect and had more freedom than women in central and southern Europe and probably elsewhere at the time, Birgit Sawyer (2003) points out that "[f]ew scholars still accept that interpretation of Germanic and Scandinavian society, yet belief in free Nordic women has lasted better and continues to influence discussions of the period" (295). Indeed, three years after Sawyer's article, Magnus Magnusson (2006) wrote:

> Women in the Viking Age played an unusually positive role in society by medieval standards. They were feisty frontierswomen in spirit and action, and in almost every respect held equal status with their menfolk. They had complete authority over all household matters, and had "liberated" legal rights far in advance of the times, such as the right to divorce and a claim to half the marital property. They made their presence felt—often, quite literally, with a vengeance. (7)

How the Story Became Popular

Within the last three or four centuries, many Sagas of Icelanders have been translated into English and other languages. These sources provide a colorful, detailed, and seductively realistic description of everyday life in the late Viking Age, even though they were recorded a couple of centuries after the end of the Viking Age. Accordingly, scholars came to rely on them as historical sources, and no other sources have had more of an impact on shaping conceptions of women and their roles than the Sagas of Icelanders.

Although women do not figure prominently in the Sagas of Icelanders, some of the women mentioned truly stand out. These are the strong, willful, domineering women who, according to the sagas, exercised rights and privileges over their own lives. They are portrayed as free to divorce and extraordinarily sensitive to the reputation of their families. It is especially when honor and vengeance on behalf of family are at stake that they assume a prominent role, and they typically do so through words with accusations of unmanliness, in order to goad men into action on their behalf. An example of such a woman is Gudrun in *Laxdæla saga* (the *Saga of the People of Laxardal*). After Kjartan, Gudrun's former lover, had disgraced her and her family, she incited her brothers to make an attack on Kjartan:

> With your temperament, you'd have made some farmer a good group of daughters, fit to do no one any good or any harm. After all the abuse and shame Kjartan has heaped upon you, you don't let it disturb your sleep while he goes riding under your very noses, with only one other man to accompany him. Such men have no better memory than a pig. There's not much chance you'll ever dare to make a move against Kjartan at home if you won't stand up to him now, when he only has one or two others to back him up. The lot of you just sit here at home, making much of yourselves, and one could only wish there were fewer of you. (Kunz 1997, 77)

Inspired no doubt by the feminist movement in the 1960s and 1970s, archaeologists, runologists, historians, and literary historians have paid much attention to women in the Viking Age. Many articles and books have been devoted to the study of women in Viking Age Scandinavia and in the decades immediately following. None of the authors denies the fact that there was no such thing as gender equality in the Viking Age, but a tendency in many of these works is to focus on women from the upper stratum of society—for the simple reason that they were the ones who were commemorated—and ignore the blacksmith's wife, the baker's wife, and the wife of the crofter, who occupied less-exalted positions and therefore left little or no legacy in the archaeological, runological, historical, and literary sources.

Archaeologists have drawn attention to the ninth-century Oseberg burial mound just south of Oslo, Norway, and pointed to the mound as the summit of status among women in Viking Age Scandinavia. Excavations of the mound, which began in 1904, revealed among other things a ship, a wagon, four sledges, skeletons of twelve horses, and, more importantly, two female skeletons (see chapter 3). One of the women was clearly quite elderly, whereas the other was considerably younger. It is possible that the younger woman was a servant and sacrificed to accompany the older woman in death. Considering the finds, which also include beds, a chair, lamps, chests, culinary implements, food, looms, combs, and shoes, it is believed that this was the burial site of a queen and her servant.

Runologists have drawn attention to runestones in Scandinavia that indicate some women enjoyed freedom and wealth. A famous example is the runestone from Dynna, just north of Oslo, Norway. It was erected by a mother in memory of her daughter. The mother clearly had the means not only to erect a runestone but also to build a bridge. The runestone has the following inscription: "Gunnvor, Thydrik's daughter, made a bridge in memory of her daughter Astrid. She was the most skillful girl in Hadeland" (R. I. Page 1987, 52). Another famous example is the runestone from Hassmyra in Västmanland, Sweden, which was raised by a man in memory of his wife. The runestone has the following inscription: "A better housewife will never come to Hassmyre to run the farm. Red Balli carved these runes. She was a good sister to Sigmund" (Jesch 1991, 650). Birgit Sawyer (2000) has advanced the theory that many of the runic inscriptions reflect claims to property by inheritance and argues that the hypothesis "is greatly strengthened by those that name women among the sponsors; it is difficult to see in what context other than the ownership of property women were often omitted from the close family circles described in the inscriptions but were sometimes included, occasionally to the exclusion of all others" (48). She mentions as an example the Hillersjö inscription (U 29):

> Read! Germund got Gerlög, a maiden, as wife. Then they had a son before he (Germund) was drowned and then the son died. Thereafter she got Gudrik as her husband. He . . . this . . . [damaged part; the reference is probably to Gudrik as the owner of Hillersjö]. Then they had children but

only one girl survived, her name was Inga. Ragnfast of Snottsta got her as wife. Thereafter he died and then the son. And the mother (Inga) inherited from her son. Then she had Erik as her husband. Then she died. Then Gerlög inherited from Inga, her daughter. Torbjörn the skald carved the runes. (Sawyer 2000, 49–50)

Accordingly, the widow Gerlög ended up inheriting from three different families.

Historians have drawn attention to legal texts and note that in some areas of Scandinavia, women clearly enjoyed more legal protection in terms of inheritance rights than had hitherto been assumed. Peter Foote and David M. Wilson (1970) note that while in Iceland, Norway, and Sweden a woman was excluded from inheritance, the law was changed in Denmark, so that the inheritance between brother and sister was equal. Although it is not known when the change took place, Foote and Wilson comment that the Danish law spread to the rest of Scandinavia. They also mention as an aside note that "in the small south Swedish province of Värend daughters and sons had equal rights as heirs, a practice contrary to all the other Scandinavian rules and one which the promulgation of a National Law for the whole of Sweden was not able to eradicate" (109).

Finally, literary historians have mined the literary sources, especially the Sagas of Icelanders, and drawn attention to the fact that at least some women were free to travel abroad and also that some women, especially widows, were able to claim land and establish farms. An often-quoted and famous example is Unn (alternatively called Aud) the Deep-Minded, wife of a Norse king in Dublin and daughter of a Norwegian chieftain, who went to the Hebrides as an agent for the Norwegian Harald Fairhair, who reigned from ca. 860 to ca. 880. Around 900, Unn's husband was killed in battle in Ireland, and her son was killed fighting in Scotland. As a result, Unn was left responsible for her grandchildren. *Laxdæla saga* reports that because of the hostilities between the Scots and the Norsemen, it would be wise to immigrate to Iceland, where she had two brothers. The saga tells that:

> She had a *knorr* [a ship] built secretly in the forest. When it was finished, she made the ship ready and set out with substantial wealth. She took along all her kinsmen who were still alive, and people say that it is hard to find another example of a woman managing to escape from such a hostile situation with as much wealth and as many followers. It shows what an outstanding woman Unn was. (Kunz 1997, 3)

The saga proceeds to relate that Unn married her granddaughters to sons of prominent men in the Orkney and Faroe Islands, whose authority she escaped by continuing to Iceland, where she laid claim to a large area of land. She gave portions of that land to family members and their followers. She didn't die until she had found a suitable wife for her grandson, to whom she bequeathed her property.

PRIMARY DOCUMENT
THE BURIAL AT OSEBERG (1923)

Oseberg is the richest burial from the Scandinavian Viking Age. In the burial chamber, skeletons of two women were found. The older woman has been tentatively identified with a certain Queen Ása mentioned in Snorri Sturluson's Heimskringla (Disc of the World). It is clear that a burial site as rich as the Oseberg site must have been for a member of the ruling dynasty. The following is the printed version of a lecture delivered by Norwegian archaeologist Anton Wilhelm Brøgger (1884–1951) to the members of the Viking Society in England in 1923.

The ships of the Viking Age discovered in Norway count among the few national productions of antiquity that have attained world wide celebrity. And justly so, for they not only give remarkable evidence of a unique heathen burial custom, but they also bear witness to a very high culture which cannot fail to be of interest to the world outside. The Oseberg discoveries, the most remarkable and abundant antiquarian find in Norway, contain a profusion of art, a wealth of objects and phenomena, coming from a people who just at that time, the ninth century, began to come into contact with one-half of Europe. It was a great period and it has given us great monuments. We have long been acquainted with its literature. Such a superb production as Egil Skallagrimson's Sonartorrek, which is one hundred years later than the Oseberg material, is a worthy companion to it.

The Oseberg ship was dug out of the earth and caused the greatest astonishment even among Norwegians. Who could know that on that spot, an out of the way barrow on the farm of Oseberg in the parish of Slagen, a little to the north of Tonsberg, there would be excavated the finest and most abundant antiquarian discoveries of Norway. It was in the summer of the year 1903 that a farmer at Oseberg began to dig the barrow. He struck some woodwork and stopped digging. A journey to Christiania brought him in touch with Professor G. Gustafson, at that time director of the University Collection of Antiquities, to whom he made known his discovery. Gustafson at once went to the spot, and made a small trial excavation, which after a day or so convinced him that the barrow contained a Viking ship, as large as the Gokstad ship excavated near Sandefjord in 1880. On that hypothesis he was able to plan his excavations, which took place throughout the summer of 1904, and were not concluded until late in the autumn. The task was long and difficult, but the result was a complete romance. That such an achievement was made, and that the Oseberg discoveries obtained so great historical importance are very largely due to the enormous care and energy displayed by Professor Gustafson. He did not live to see the completion of the work of preparing the material discovered, dying in the midst of his labors in April, 1915.

The barrow in which the discovery was made was situated close to an ancient river bed, five kilometers from the sea. During the Viking Age the river was navigable for a vessel of the size of the Oseberg ship. The barrow was at one time one of the largest in Norway, but in the course of centuries had been completely destroyed. It was built of huge masses of peat, and formed a completely airtight covering over the whole of the interior, and in conjunction with the foundation of clay in which all the objects lay, it resulted in the excellent state of preservation which characterizes the material excavated. All the wooden objects were preserved, although broken by mechanical means, through the great pressure of the masses of earth above.

The ship lay in the barrow pointing north to south, with the prow toward the south. Behind the mast there was a sepulchral chamber of timber in which lay the dead. Stones were thrown over the whole of the ship, and above them the barrow was erected. At the very commencement of the excavations, those engaged found proofs that the barrow had been broken into in ancient times, and the course of the thieves could be distinctly traced. From the southern side of the mound they penetrated to the middle by means of an open passage some three or four meters in breadth, with the sole object of reaching the sepulchral chamber. It was evident that they had succeeded in doing so, for the chamber bore very distinct traces of their work. They chopped out a large opening in the tent-shaped roof, and took away a considerable quantity of the valuables which must undoubtedly have been in the chamber. This compartment contained the bodies of two women, the Oseberg Queen and her bond-woman. We can see how the robbers desecrated the corpses by chopping off arms and hands which presumably bore gold rings. Traces of the robbers were found all over the passages along which they had forced an entrance. Here and there lay broken remains of objects which had lain in the sepulchral chamber.

From the level of the thieves' entrance an investigation was by degrees made of the sepulchral chamber. There had lain the two dead women, presumably each in a separate bed, surrounded by coverlets, pillows, and clothes. One of the women, perhaps the Queen herself, must have been about thirty years of age, the other about fifty. The sepulchral chamber in the ship was made their resting place, and with them were placed a number of articles of a more personal character. We must content ourselves by mentioning the most important. There was a beautiful oak chest containing both fruit and grain, viz., wild apples (crab-apples) and wheat. Wild apples were found in other parts of the ship, and in all we have now about fifty of them. We may here mention that the vegetable remains from the Oseberg ship are in such considerable quantities, that they prove with certainty that, assuming the year to have been a normal one from the point of view of vegetation, the burial of the Oseberg Queen must have taken place at the end of August or during the first week of September.

Two other chests were found in the chamber, both of oak. One of them was quite entire, and contained two iron lamps with long rods, a wooden box for cotton, an awl, a spindle, iron scissors, horseshoe nails, etc. In general, the sepulchral chamber contained a collection of domestic implements. We may mention a winder for yarn, and also two looms, both of very important and interesting types. In this connection we may also mention the most remarkable contents of the sepulchral chamber, the numerous remnants of woven picture tapestries which lay there. At the present time a scientific assistant to the Editorial Committee is working at this material, and it may be said, *inter alia*, that these tapestries must to a large extent have been made in Norway.

In another part of the sepulchral chamber was found a collection of buckets and pails. Two of these belong to the most beautiful objects in the entire collection, one having four handles and a wealth of brass fittings, the unique form of which has given rise to the incorrect name "Buddha" pail, whereas the workmanship is Western and most probably English, belonging to the early Viking period.

It should also be mentioned that the sepulchral chamber once contained two beds, a large quantity of rope for tents and sails, a considerable quantity of down and feathers for pillows and coverlets, a number of unique and beautifully carved wooden poles representing the heads of animals, and further a quantity of large and small objects of various kinds.

When the investigation of the sepulchral chamber was completed, it was possible to proceed with the stern of the ship. The space was small, but nevertheless it contained a number of the objects belonging to a tidy and well-appointed kitchen, such as an iron pot with a three-legged stand, a chain for a hanging pot, a number of small dishes and troughs of wood, frying pans, kit-boxes, knives, a hand-mill for corn, a kitchen stool with four legs, and a great many other articles. In the stern there also lay a small axe. It was placed between two oak planks and was wonderfully well preserved.

That which was found in the sepulchral chamber and in the stern, however, was nothing in comparison with that found in the fore part of the ship. It is only possible to enumerate here the most important of the objects discovered. As regards ships' equipment here were found a number of oars, a gangway plank, two water barrels, booms and gaffs for spreading sails, bailing scoops, anchors and anchor stocks, in addition to a number of indeterminate objects which undoubtedly belong to the equipment of a ship. Among the burial equipment may be mentioned, first and foremost, the beautiful four-wheeled wagon, which is one of the most remarkable objects in the Oseberg collection. As will be seen, it was intended to be drawn by two horses, and has a most curious construction, there being a loose wagon body made of oak. On the sides of the latter we find some very interesting and remarkable carvings in the oak. As regards other vehicles, there were four sledges, three of which are very beautiful and luxurious, with richly carved bodies. These, too, were intended for two horses. There were also discovered three beds, the framework for two tents, one framework for a very large tent, a chair, a trough containing rye flour, several wooden dishes, a box or basket made of bast, two buckets, one of which contained combs, balls of thread, wax, buckles, mountings, and in addition seeds of the woad plant which was used for dyeing, and also flax seeds and wild apples. There were further a litter or stretcher, a number of spades, three pairs of shoes, a ribbon loom, a beautifully carved pole representing an animal's head, three sledge poles, harness for horses and chains for dogs. Finally, in addition to all the above, there were the remains of fifteen horses, four dogs and an ox. It was certainly not a cheap funeral!

In the fore part of the vessel oars had been stuck out through openings in the ship's side ready for the voyage. In other words, it was intended that the Queen should be able to use the ship just as she had done during her lifetime.

It was not until the end of September, 1904, that all the different objects had been excavated, and for the first time since its burial the Oseberg ship lay uncovered. It was not a pleasing sight, twisted as it was by the masses of earth, the bottom of the ship pushed up by the underlying clay, broken, warped, all the boards crushed and loosened, the ribs sundered and partly destroyed. The ship required to be taken out as quickly as possible, but that could of course not be done except piece by piece. An expert ships' engineer supervised the work, which proceeded until the Oseberg ship, in about 2,000 pieces, reached Christiania at the end of December, 1904. There it was at first stored, and then, after a lengthy restoration, was re-erected on the spot where it stands today.

The Oseberg ship itself is a large, open boat, twenty meters long on her keel, and about twenty-four meters from stem to stern. The breadth is very great, being more than five meters, and the vessel is quite flat-bottomed, being intended to sail in very shallow water. The height above the water-line is quite inappreciable. She has seventeen ribs and holds (or intermediate spaces), all the important parts being made of oak, and there are fifteen holes for oars on each side, so that thirty men were required to row the ship. But in addition she has a pine-mast for a sail. There was a deck or flooring. The ship was steered by means of a rudder placed on the starboard side aft. Thus the Oseberg ship was not a sea-going boat like the Gokstad ship), so that it would not be possible to sail to America in the Oseberg ship, as Magnus Andersen did in a replica of the Gokstad ship in 1893, although the two vessels are almost of the same size. But the reason is that the purpose of the two, vessels was different. One was a sea-going ship, the other a pleasure boat. The Oseberg ship was the Queen's yacht for summer cruises along the Norwegian coast within the sheltered waters inside the skerries. The stem and stern of the ship are richly decorated, with beautiful carvings of animals. This is the first monumental work of Norwegian art. The great profusion of art in the Oseberg discoveries represents new acquisitions for the history of Norwegian culture and is of the utmost importance. It is Norwegian in spirit and in execution. The subjects are, of course, the result of influences from various parts of Europe, but in scarcely any country of Europe can we find at that time—the decades succeeding the death of Charlemagne,—such a rich, independent, and fruitful art as that which the Oseberg discoveries have revealed to us in Norway.

There is one very natural question which every one will ask when reading of the Oseberg Queen and her treasures. Who was she? The present author, in a work published in 1915, endeavored to prove that we can connect this remarkable group of discoveries of ships with a special Norwegian princely family, that which commenced the conquest of Norway from Vestfold. By means of detailed investigations, which space does not permit us to refer to here, the author has tried to show that the Oseberg Queen must be a certain Queen Asa, who was the mother of King Halfdan the Black, and also the grandmother of King Harald the Fairhaired. She was married to King Godrod in Vestfold, but against her will. The year after Halfdan was born she caused her husband to be killed in revenge for his having taken away and killed her father and brother. It is on account of this fearful deed that her name is preserved in our history. But she was a remarkable woman, loved and feared. She brought up her son Halfdan the Black, and gave him lofty ideals regarding his vocation. Her figure stands out in history as fully worthy of the picture we obtain of her by means of the Oseberg discoveries.

Source: Brøgger, Anton Wilhelm. 1921. "The Oseberg Ship." *Saga-Book* 10 (1928–1929): 1–11. Used by permission of the Viking Society for Northern Research.

What Really Happened

While it is true that some women in Viking Age Scandinavia and Iceland were respected and appear to have had few restraints on their activity and freedom, the picture of the woman that emerges from the Sagas of Icelanders is not a realistic one. The (Christian) composers of the Sagas of Icelanders, which for the most part deals with the heathen past of Icelanders and Norwegians, had their own agendas and subjected the descriptions of women to their own special purposes. As Sawyer (2003) points out, in these sagas, "we often meet women as inciters, dangerous opponents and skilled in magic, and far from representing ideal women, they illustrate the ecclesiastical image of woman as a threat and danger to men" (297). Sagas written about contemporary conditions in late medieval Iceland, such as *Sturlunga saga* (the *Saga of the Sturlungs*), a huge compilation of sagas from around 1300, which provides a detailed and apparently reliable picture of the attitudes and values of the time, do not in their descriptions of women corroborate the existence of strong and independent women. Women hardly figure in *Sturlunga saga*, and what may be gleaned from the scant mention of them is that they had no say in terms of marriage; men arranged the marriages of their womenfolk—daughters, sisters, sisters-in-law, and so on—according to their own economic and political interests. Moreover, medieval Icelandic laws do not confirm the easy divorce mentioned in the Sagas of Icelanders. The general picture that may be obtained from *Sturlunga saga* and other contemporary sagas is that of a subservient, submissive woman, whose place was in the home, managing those affairs that pertained within the house and its immediate vicinity. The affairs included the preparation and preservation of food and drink, cleaning and laundering, and the manufacturing of cloth and the production of garments or hangings. Her primary duty was to provide her husband with offspring, and the care of infants and small children must have occupied much of a woman's time. The keys at her girdle were a sign of her authority, at least in the house, and some very finely made keys have been found in Viking Age women's graves in Norway (for examples, see Lars Jørgensen 2000, 84). As Jochens (1986) points out, there is very little evidence in the contemporary sagas that women took the initiative or were involved in men's affairs.

Also, it is known from late-medieval Scandinavian and Icelandic sources that women had no political rights. In Iceland, a woman could not serve as a chieftain (*goði*), could not be a judge, could not be a witness, and could not speak at assemblies. If a woman wanted to initiate or conduct legal proceedings, a man would have to do so on her behalf. Typically, a woman had limited opportunity to dispose of property and could not inherit if she had brothers to take over the family inheritance. A woman was, by law, under the authority of her father, her husband, or her sons.

Moreover, it should be mentioned that polygamy seems to have been fairly common in Viking Age Scandinavia. In his *Gesta Hammaburgensis ecclesiae pontificum* (*Activities of the Prelates of the Church of Hamburg*), the 11th-century cleric Adam of Bremen writes about the Swedes that "in their sexual relations with women . . . they know no bounds; a man according to his means has two or three or more wives at one time, rich men and princes an unlimited number" (1959, 203). The Norwegian Earl Hakon of Lade (d. c. 995), for example, reportedly had the daughters of his subjects brought home to him, where he slept with them for a week or two and then sent them back to their parents. Women, on the other hand, were punished, if they had extramarital affairs. According to some of the Danish and Swedish provincial laws, it gave a husband the right to kill his wife and her lover if they were caught in the act.

Obviously, it is wrong to think of women in Viking Age Scandinavia and Iceland as a monolithic group. The Viking Age spanned three centuries, and during that time, northern Europe underwent many changes. Moreover, Scandinavia is a vast area. Accordingly, the life of a farmer's wife in northern Norway was very different from the life of a trader's wife in southern Denmark. However, common to the vast majority of women in Viking Age Scandinavia is that their primary functions were as wives and mothers. Women did not hold sway with men, and there was no such thing as equal gender rights.

PRIMARY DOCUMENT

SAGA OF THE PEOPLE OF LAXARDAL (CA. 1250)

This excerpt from Laxdæla saga (*the* Saga of the People of Laxardal), *composed in Iceland around the middle of the 13th century, relates that Höskuld, a well-known and wealthy Icelander purchased a mute slave woman from a Rus merchant while on a royal expedition. He made her his concubine and brought her back to Iceland—much to the chagrin of Jorun, his wife.*

Chapter 12

There were tidings at the beginning of the summer that the king went with his fleet eastward to a tryst in Brenn-isles, to settle peace for his land, even as the law laid down should be done every third summer. This meeting was held between rulers with a view to settling such matters as kings had to adjudge—matters of international policy between Norway, Sweden, and Denmark. It was deemed a pleasure trip to go to this meeting, for thither came men from well-nigh all such lands as we know of. Hoskuld ran out his ship, being desirous also to go to the meeting; moreover, he had not been to see the king all the winter through. There was also a fair to be made for. At the meeting there were great crowds of people, and much amusement to be got—drinking, and games, and all sorts of entertainment. Nought, however, of great interest happened there. Hoskuld met many of his kinsfolk there who were come from Denmark. Now, one day as Hoskuld went out to disport himself with some other men, he saw a stately tent far away from the other booths. Hoskuld went thither, and into the tent, and there sat a man before him in costly raiment, and a Russian hat on his head. Hoskuld asked him his name.

He said he was called Gilli: "But many call to mind the man if they hear my nickname—I am called Gilli the Russian."

Hoskuld said he had often heard talk of him, and that he held him to be the richest of men that had ever be longed to the guild of merchants. Still Hoskuld spoke: "You must have things to sell such as we should wish to buy."

Gilli asked what he and his companions wished to buy. Hoskuld said he should like to buy some bondswoman, "if you have one to sell."

Gilli answers: "There, you mean to give me trouble by this, in asking for things you don't expect me to have in stock; but it is not sure that that follows."

Hoskuld then saw that right across the booth there was drawn a curtain; and Gilli then lifted the curtain, and Hoskuld saw that there were twelve women seated behind the curtain. So Gilli said that Hoskuld should come on and have a look, if he would care to buy any of these women. Hoskuld did so. They sat all together across the booth. Hoskuld looks carefully at these women. He saw a woman sitting out by the skirt of the tent, and she was very ill-clad. Hoskuld thought, as far as he could see, this woman was fair to look upon. Then said Hoskuld, "What is the price of that woman if I should wish to buy her?"

Gilli replied, "Three silver pieces is what you must weigh me out for her."

"It seems to me," said Hoskuld, "that you charge very highly for this bondswoman, for that is the price of three (such)."

Then Gilli said, "You speak truly, that I value her worth more than the others. Choose any of the other eleven, and pay one mark of silver for her, this one being left in my possession."

Hoskuld said, "I must first see how much silver there is in the purse I have on my belt," and he asked Gilli to take the scales while he searched the purse.

Gilli then said, "On my side there shall be no guile in this matter; for, as to the ways of this woman, there is a great drawback which I wish, Hoskuld, that you know before we strike this bargain."

Hoskuld asked what it was.

Gilli replied, "The woman is dumb. I have tried in many ways to get her to talk, but have never got a word out of her, and I feel quite sure that this woman knows not how to speak."

Then, said Hoskuld, "Bring out the scales, and let us see how much the purse I have got here may weigh."

Gilli did so, and now they weigh the silver, and there were just three marks weighed. Then said Hoskuld, "Now the matter stands so that we can close our bargain. You take the money for yourself, and I will take the woman. I take it that you have behaved honestly in this affair, for, to be sure, you had no mind to deceive me herein."

Hoskuld then went home to his booth. That same night Hoskuld went into bed with her. The next morning when men got dressed, spake Hoskuld, "The clothes Gilli the Rich gave you do not appear to be very grand, though it is true that to him it is more of a task to dress twelve women than it is to me to dress only one."

After that Hoskuld opened a chest, and took out some fine women's clothes and gave them to her; and it was the saying of every one that she looked very well when she was dressed. But when the rulers had there talked matters over according as the law provided, this meeting was broken up. Then Hoskuld went to see King Hakon, and greeted him worthily, according to custom. The king cast a side glance at him, and said, "We should have taken well your greeting, Hoskuld, even if you had saluted us sooner; but so shall it be even now."

Chapter 13

After that the king received Hoskuld most graciously, and bade him come on board his own ship, and "be with us so long as you care to remain in Norway."

Hoskuld answered: "Thank you for your offer; but now, this summer, I have much to be busy about, and that is mostly the reason I was so long before I came to see you, for I wanted to get for myself house-timber."

The king bade him bring his ship in to the Wick, and Hoskuld tarried with the king for a while. The king got house-timber for him, and had his ship laden for him. Then the king said to Hoskuld, "You shall not be delayed here longer than you like, though we shall find it difficult to find a man to take your place."

After that the king saw Hoskuld off to his ship, and said: "I have found you an honourable man, and now my mind misgives me that you are sailing for the last time from Norway, whilst I am lord over that land."

The king drew a gold ring off his arm that weighed a mark, and gave it to Hoskuld; and he gave him for lip another gift a sword on which there was half a mark of gold. Hoskuld thanked the king for his gifts, and for all the honour he had done him. After that Hoskuld went on board his ship, and put to sea. They had a fair wind, and hove in to the south of Iceland; and after that sailed west by Reekness, and so by Snowfellness in to Broadfirth. Hoskuld landed at Salmon-river-Mouth. He had the cargo taken out of his ship, which he took into the river and beached, having a shed built for it. A ruin is to be seen now where he built the shed. There he set up his booths, and that place is called Booths'-Dale. After that Hoskuld had the timber taken home, which was very easy, as it was not far off. Hoskuld rode home after that with a few men, and was warmly greeted, as was to be looked for. He found that all his belongings had been kept well since he left. Jorunn asked, "What woman that was who journeyed with him?"

Hoskuld answered, "You will think I am giving you a mocking answer when I tell you that I do not know her name."

Jorunn said, "One of two things there must be: either the talk is a lie that has come to my ears, or you must have spoken to her so much as to have asked her her name."

Hoskuld said he could not gainsay that, and so told her the truth, and bade that the woman should be kindly treated, and said it was his wish she should stay in service with them.

Jorunn said, "I am not going to wrangle with the mistress you have brought out of Norway, should she find living near me no pleasure; least of all should I think of it if she is both deaf and dumb."

Hoskuld slept with his wife every night after he came home, and had very little to say to the mistress. Every one clearly saw that there was something betokening high birth in the way she bore herself, and that she was no fool. Towards the end of the winter Hoskuld's mistress gave birth to a male child. Hoskuld was called, and was shown the child, and he thought, as others did, that he had never seen a goodlier or a more noble-looking child. Hoskuld was asked what the boy should be called. He said it should be named Olaf, for Olaf Feilan had died a little time before, who was his mother's brother. Olaf was far before other children, and Hoskuld bestowed great love on the boy. The next summer Jorunn said, "That the woman must do some work or other, or else go away."

Hoskuld said she should wait on him and his wife, and take care of her boy besides. When the boy was two years old he had got full speech, and ran about like children of four years old. Early one morning, as Hoskuld had gone out to look about his manor, the weather being fine, and the sun, as yet little risen in the sky, shining brightly, it happened that he heard some voices of people talking; so he went down to where a little brook ran past the home-field slope, and he saw two people there whom he recognised as his son Olaf and his mother, and he discovered she was not speechless, for she was talking a great deal to the boy. Then Hoskuld went to her and asked her her name, and said it was useless for her to hide it any longer. She said so it should be, and they sat down on the brink of the field.

Then she said, "If you want to know my name, I am called Melkorka."

Hoskuld bade her tell him more of her kindred. she answered, "Myr Kjartan is the name of my father, and he is a king in Ireland; and I was taken a prisoner of war from there when I was fifteen winters old."

Hoskuld said she had kept silence far too long about so noble a descent. After that Hoskuld went on, and told Jorunn what he had just found out during his walk. Jorunn said that she "could not tell if this were true," and said she had no fondness for any manner of wizards; and so the matter dropped. Jorunn was no kinder to her than before, but Hoskuld had somewhat more to say to her. A little while after this, when Jorunn was going to bed, Melkorka was undressing her, and put her shoes on the floor, when Jorunn took the stockings and smote her with them about the head. Melkorka got angry, and struck Jorunn on the nose with her fist, so that the blood flowed. Hoskuld came in and parted them. After that he let Melkorka go away, and got a dwelling ready for her up in Salmon-river-Dale, at the place that was afterwards called Melkorkastead, which is now waste land on the south of the Salmon river. Melkorka now set up household there, and Hoskuld had everything brought there that she needed; and Olaf, their son, went with her. It was soon seen that Olaf, as he grew up, was far superior to other men, both on account of his beauty and courtesy.

Source: Press, Muriel A. C., trans. 1899. *Laxdæla Saga*. London: Dent. 21–28.

Further Reading

Adam of Bremen. 1959. *History of the Archbishops of Hamburg-Bremen*, translated by Francis J. Tschan. Records of Civilization: Sources and Studies 53. New York: Columbia University Press.

Foote, Peter, and David M. Wilson. 1970. *The Viking Achievement: The Society and Culture of Early Medieval Scandinavia*. London: Sidgwick & Jackson.

Jesch, Judith. 1991. *Women in the Viking Age*. Woodbridge: The Boydell Press.

Jochens, Jenny. 1986. "The Medieval Icelandic Heroine: Fact or Fiction?" *Viator* 17: 35–50.

Jørgensen, Lars. 2000. "Political Organization and Social Life." In *Vikings: The North Atlantic Saga*, edited by William W. Fitzhugh and Elizabeth I. Ward. Washington: Smithsonian Institution Press. 72–85.

Kunz, Keneva, trans. 1997. "The Saga of the People of Laxardal." In *The Complete Sagas of Icelanders Including 49 Tales*, 5 vols. Volume 5. Reykjavik: Leifur Eiríksson Publishing. 1–120.

Magnusson, Magnus. 2006. "Foreword." In *The Vikings: Voyagers of Discovery and Plunder*, edited by René Chartrand, Keith Durham, Mark Harrison, Ian Heath, and Magnus Magnusson. Oxford: Osprey Publishing. 6–8.

Page, R. I. 1987. *Runes*. London: British Museum Publications.
"Remarks by First Lady Hillary Rodham Clinton." 1999. *National Museum of Natural History*. April 8. Accessed September 28, 2017. https://naturalhistory.si.edu/exhibits/vikings/firstlady.html.
Sawyer, Birgit. 2000. *The Viking-Age Rune-Stones: Custom and Commemoration in Early Medieval Scandinavia*. Oxford: Oxford University Press.
Sawyer, Birgit. 2003. "Women in Viking-Age Scandinavia, or, Who Were the 'Shieldmaidens'?" In *Vínland Revisited: The Norse World at the Turn of the First Millennium: Selected Papers from the Viking Millennium International Symposium, 15–24 September 2000, Newfoundland and Labrador*, edited by Shannon Lewis-Simpson. St. John's: Historic Sites Association of Newfoundland and Labrador.

7

Vikings Had Primitive Weapons

What People Think Happened

Some people believe that Vikings used unsophisticated or primitive weapons in their attacks, such as clubs and low-quality axes. Although it is difficult to exactly pinpoint the origin of this misunderstanding, those affected by Viking raiding activity likely played a key role in negative portrayals of the Norse. One source for the idea that the Vikings used primitive weapons, such as clubs, could possibly be the *Passion of Saint Edmund, King and Martyr*. Edmund was the king of the East Angles from 855 until 870, when he was captured by the Danes and killed. In its characteristically terse style, the *Anglo-Saxon Chronicle* only makes brief mention of the event: "and in that year St Edmund the king fought against [the Viking army], and the Danish took the victory, and killed the king" (Swanton 2000, 71).

However, the *Passion of Saint Edmund*, an Old English translation by the Anglo-Saxon monk Aelfric of Eynsham of the French abbot Abbo of Fleury's Latin *Passio Sancti Eadmundi*, describes the event in detail. King Edmund received an ultimatum to submit to the Danes but refused. After having laid down his weapons to become a martyr, he was captured by the Vikings and beaten with clubs before being decapitated. However, it is important to consider that Aelfric lived in the late 10th century, and the Latin original from which he translated dates to around 986, more than one hundred years after the events described. Considering the fact that the *Anglo-Saxon Chronicle* does not explicitly describe Edmund's death at the hands of the Danes, the detail of the king beaten with clubs might be a later embellishment to emphasize Edmund's holiness and similarity to Christ. Nevertheless, the details stuck and were perpetuated in later documents. The manuscript Morgan M.736 (*Miscellany on the Life of St. Edmund*) from approximately 1130, which is located in the Morgan Library in New York, contains numerous illuminations, including three (on folios 12v, 13r and 13v) depicting Edmund being beaten with clubs. Likewise, the later manuscript British Library Harley 2278 from 1433–1434 contains two scenes (on folios 060v and 062r) of Edmund being brutalized by Norsemen with clubs before being decapitated.

How the Story Became Popular

The surprise attacks of the Vikings on Anglo-Saxon monasteries and settlements in the eighth century understandably shocked and traumatized their victims, which likely aided in the creation the image of the "primitive" Norseman (see chapter 3). In Aelfric's *Passion of Saint Edmund*, the Vikings are described as "savage," "bloodthirsty," "wicked," "like [wolves]," and "associated by the devil," (Skeat 1900, 317, 319, 321), which probably echoes sentiment by others visited by the Norse on their raiding campaigns. It would seem logical for the Vikings, who in the eyes of their enemies were evil and even demonic, to wield crude, brutish weapons while carrying out their brutish acts.

Although composed at a much later date, an episode in *Laxdæla saga* (the *Saga of the People of Laxardal*) may have contributed to the notion that Vikings had poor-quality weapons. The episode in question describes Kjartan's last battle, and it relates that his sword kept getting bent out of shape: "Kjartan struck powerful blows, which proved to be more than his sword could bear, and more often than once he had to straighten it by standing on it" (Kunz 1997, 51). Nineteenth-century saga scholarship accepted the Old Norse-Icelandic sagas as historical fact, and so this incident in *Laxdæla saga* could possibly have led scholars to believe that the Norse had crude weapons.

Popular culture has had quite a hand in perpetuating the idea that Vikings had low-quality weapons. The 1928 film *The Viking*, directed by Roy William Neill and based on the 1902 novel *The Thrall of Leif the Lucky* by Ottilie A. Liljencrantz, shows the Norse in unmitigated barbarian mode in some of the scenes, with horned and winged helmets; thick, wild beards and unkempt long hair; half-naked and wrapped only in crude fur tunics and loincloths, evoking frenzied cavemen. They wield swords, axes, and clubs; even a pitchfork is discernable in the first raid scene. In this movie, the Norse are truly depicted as a primitive people, wielding whatever kinds of weapons they could get their hands on. In the 1964 film *The Long Ships*, directed by Jack Cardiff, the Vikings are also shown wielding clubs, planks, and huge, unhistorical double-sided axes in addition to swords and relatively historical axes. In 1966, René Goscinny and Albert Uderzo released the ninth book in the *Astérix* comic series, *Astérix et les Normands*, which was translated and released in 1978 with the English title *Asterix and the Normans*. In this book, the Vikings are depicted wearing fur clothing and horned helmets. In addition, a spiked wooden club seems to be among their standard equipment, appearing numerous times alongside axes and swords. The 1972–1974 German-Austrian-Japanese-produced animated TV series *Vicky the Viking* (German/Austrian: *Wickie und die starken Männer*, Japanese: *Chiisana Viking Bikke*) based on Runer Johnson's *Vicke Viking*, in an interesting twist, depicts only the villains, Sven the Terrible and his men, wielding ball-and-chain flails and morning stars alongside swords, while Vicky and the heroes only use bladed weapons. In 2009, a live-action film based on the series, also titled *Vicky the Viking* (*Wickie und die starken Männer*), was released in Germany and garnered huge success. The film was faithful to the animated series in all its details, including the weaponry used by each side. In 1973, Dik Browne created the comic "Hagar the Horrible," whose main character, Hagar, is usually shown with a stubby, well-worn sword. Considering the many depictions in popular culture of the Norse as barbarians, it is understandable how the misconception of their primitive weapons became rooted in people's minds.

PRIMARY DOCUMENTS

AELFRIC OF EYNSHAM'S *PASSION OF SAINT EDMUND* (11TH CENTURY)

The excerpt from Aelfric of Eynsham's Passion of Saint Edmund, King and Martyr, *describes King Edmund's meeting with the Danish leader Hingwar, who has been identified with Ivar the Boneless, the son of Ragnar Shaggy-Breeches, and subsequent martyrdom in 870. Aelfric's Old English text is a translation from the 986 Latin account by Abbo of Fleury. The text, which tells of the Danes beating King Edmund with clubs before decapitating him, might be one of the earliest mentions of Vikings using crude, primitive weapons. It should be noted that this medieval text also expresses anti-Semitic sentiment, which was a common reality even within learned discourse during the Middle Ages.*

Edmund the blessed, king of the East Angles,
was wise and honourable, and ever glorified,
by his excellent conduct, Almighty God.
He was humble and devout, and continued so steadfast
that he would not yield to shameful sins,
nor in any direction did he bend aside his practices,
but was always mindful of the true doctrine.
[If] thou art made a chief man, exalt not thyself,
but amongst men as one of them.
He was bountiful to the poor and to widows even like a father,
and with benignity guided his people
ever to righteousness, and controlled the violent,
and lived happily in the true faith.
Then at last it befell that the Danish people
came with a fleet, harrying and slaying
widely over the land, as their custom is.
In that fleet were their chief men,
Hingwar and Hubba, associated by the devil,
and they landed in Northumbria with their ships,
and wasted the land and slew the people.
Then Hingwar turned eastward with his ships,
and Hubba was left in Northumbria,
having won the victory by means of cruelty.
Then Hingwar came rowing to East Anglia
in the year when Ælfred the ætheling was one and twenty years old,
he who afterward became the renowned kind of the West-Saxons.
And the aforesaid Hingwar suddenly, like a wolf,
stalked over the land and slew the people,
men and women, and witless children,
and shamefully tormented the innocent Christians.
Then soon afterward he sent to the king
a threatening message, that he must bow down
to do him homage, if he recked of his life.
So the messenger came to king Edmund,
and speedily announced to him Hingwar's message.
'Hingwar out king, keen and victorious
by sea and by land, hath rule over many peoples,
and has landed here suddenly even now with an army,
that he may take up his winter-quarters here with his host.
Now he commandeth thee to divide thy secret treasures
and thine ancestors' wealth quickly with him,

and thou shalt be his under-king, if thou desire to live,
because thou hast not the power that thou mayst withstand him.'
So then king Edmund called a bishop
who was handiest to him, and consulted with him
how he should answer the savage Hingwar.
Then the bishop feared for this terrible misfortune,
and for the king's life, and said that it seemed best to him
that he should submit to that which Hingwar bade him.
Then the king kept silence and looked on the ground,
and said to him at last even like a king;
'Behold, thou bishop, the poor people of this land
are brought to shame, and it were now dearer to me
that I should fall in fight against him who would possess
my people's inheritance.' And the bishop said,
'Alas, thou dear king thy people lie slain,
and thou hast not sufficient forces with which thou mayest fight,
and these seamen will come and will bind thee alive,
unless thou save thy life by means of flight,
or thus save thyself by yielding to him.'
Then said Edmund the king, full brave as he was;
'This I desire and wish in my mind,
that I should not be left alone after my dear thanes,
who even in their beds, with their bairns and their wives,
have by these seamen been suddenly slain.
It was never my custom to take to flight,
but I would rather die, if I must,
for my own land; and almighty God knoweth
that I will never turn aside from His worship,
nor from His true love, whether I die or live.'
After these words he turned to the messenger
whom Hingwar had sent to him, and said to him undismayed:
'Verily thou wouldest now be worthy of death,
but I will not defile my clean hands
with thy foul blood, because I follow Christ,
who hath so given us an example, and I will blithely
be slain by you, if God hath so ordained.
Depart not very quickly, and say to thy cruel lord;
Edmund the king will never bow in life to Hingwar
the heathen leader, unless he will first bow,
in this land, to Jesus Christ with faith.'
Then went the messenger quickly away,

and met on the way the bloodthirsty Hingwar
with all his army hurrying to Edmund,
and told that wicked man how he was answered.
Hingwar then arrogantly commanded his troops
that they should, all of them, take the king alone,
who had despised his command, and instantly bind him.
Then Edmund the king, when Hingwar came,
stood within his hall mindful of the Savior,
and threw away his weapons, desiring to imitate
Christ's example, who forbade Peter
to fight with weapons against the bloodthirsty Jews.
Then those wicked men bound Edmund,
and shamefully insulted him, and beat him with clubs,
and afterward they led the faithful king
to an earth-fast tree, and tied him thereto
with hard bonds, and afterwards scourged him
a long while with whips, and ever he called,
between the blows, with true faith,
on Jesus Christ; and then the heathen
because of his faith were madly angry,
because he called upon Christ to help him.
They shot at him with javelins as if for their amusement,
until he was all beset with their shots,
as with a porcupine's bristles, even as Sebastian was.
When Hingwar, the wicked seaman,
saw that the noble king would not deny Christ,
but with steadfast faith ever called upon Him,
then he commanded men to behead him, and the heathen did so.
For while he was yet calling upon Christ,
the heathen drew away the saint, to slay him,
and with one blow struck off his head;
and his soul departed joyfully to Christ.
There was a certain man at hand, kept by God
hidden from the heathen, who heard all this,
and told it afterward even as we tell it here.
So then the seamen went again to ship,
and hid the head of the holy Edmund
in the thick brambles, that it might not be buried.

Source: Skeat, Walter W. 1900. "Passion of Saint Edmund." In *Aelfric's Lives of Saints*. The Early English Text Society, 76, 82, 94, 114, Volume 2. 314–335.

MISCELLANY ON THE LIFE OF ST. EDMUND (CA. 1130)

Edmund is shown beaten by Danes with clubs before being decapitated.

Source: Miscellany on the life of St. Edmund (MS M.736)., fol. 12v. Used by permission of the Morgan Library and Museum.

What Really Happened

The Vikings had a great variety of weapons at their disposal, ranging from simple, everyday knives and woodcutting axes to war axes, spears, javelins, and swords. Weapons, especially expensive ones of quality carrying higher prestige, were much valued. This is illustrated by the many instances in the Old Norse-Icelandic sagas where weapons bear names that describe their possessed or desired qualities. Examples include *Rimmugýgr* (*Battle-hag*) in *Njáls saga* (the *Saga of Njal*), *Brynjubítr* (*byrnie [chain mail coat]-biter*) and *Sætarspillir* (*truce-spiller, peace-breaker*) in *Sturlunga Saga* (the *Saga of the Sturlungs*), and *Fótbítr* (*foot-biter, leg-biter*) in *Laxdæla saga*. Stanza 38 in the eddic poem *Hávamál* (*Sayings of the High One* [=Odin]) mentions that a man should never be without his weapons: "From his weapons on the open road / no man should step one pace away; / you don't know for certain when you're out on the road / when you might have need of your spear" (Larrington 1996, 19). Clearly, weapons were essential to life during the Viking Age. They were not only a necessity but also a means of displaying social status.

Archaeological evidence from Viking Age burials suggests that the most common weapon was the spear (Line 2014, 27). Spears were an economic choice, since they required a relatively small amount of costly metal to produce the spearhead, and the shaft provided the wielder with a long reach. Like other wooden objects, spear poles have survived only in fragments but were apparently made of a variety of types of wood. Spear length during the Viking Age was not uniform but probably ranged from 4.9 to 9.2 feet (Line 2014, 28). The Saga of Icelanders mention six different terms for pole weapons, only some of which are tentatively identifiable with archaeological examples (Orkisz 2016, 206–207). It is clear, however, that various spears and other pole weapons could be used to throw, stab, thrust, slash, and cut opponents. Other common weapons in Viking Age Scandinavia were knives, saxes, and bows and arrows. Knives were carried by most people for everyday household and work tasks, while saxes were longer knives or short swords with a single edge, usually between 1.5 and almost three feet. Bows were used for hunting as well as battle, depending on the type of arrowhead employed (Line 2014, 28–29 and 31–32).

Axes were also a popular weapon in the Viking Age. Since axes were a conventional tool for woodcutting or other household tasks, even the poorest Viking warrior would have had access to an axe as a weapon. Several basic types of axes existed: the Danish axe, the broadaxe, and the bearded axe (Lindsay 1965, 27–28). The bearded axe was more common during the early Viking Age and earned its name because the lower part of the blade extended downward, resembling a beard. Later types are the Danish axe (also known as handaxe), which was typically light and designed for one-handed use, and the broadaxe, which was larger and sometimes two-handed, as evident from Bayeux tapestry, a nearly 75-yard-long embroidered work depicting the Norman conquest in 1066. The axe could also signal social status, and some axes were ornately decorated; an example is the Mammen axe from Denmark, which is inlaid with an intricate silver interlace design.

Swords were an elite weapon during the Viking Age, and since their production required a large amount of metal, they were also the most expensive. Swords were double-edged and typically almost three feet long. The Viking Age saw advancements in sword technology: a groove or "fuller" was added to the center of the blade to reduce its weight and increase flexibility, and the hand-guard was widened, providing more hand protection for the wielder (Pedersen 2008, 204–205). Hilts were also sometimes lavishly decorated with precious metals such as bronze, silver, and gold, signaling the high social status of the owner.

Although swords during the Early Middle Ages were expensive and high-status objects, they were usually made of relatively poor-quality steel, resulting in brittle blades that were easily damaged or even broken during combat. However, a very special type of sword was also in use in northern Europe during the Viking Age. About 170 swords of much higher quality than the typical medieval sword have been found in Scandinavia, northern Germany, France, the British Isles, and the Baltic countries, with the highest concentration in Norway, Sweden, Finland, Russia, and the eastern part of the Baltic. These exceptional weapons, known as Ulfberht swords, were produced from the mid-eighth century to the end of the 11th century (Stalsberg 2008, 8). The name Ulfberht derives from the inscription on the blades reading +VLFBERH+T, and variations thereof, which was once believed to have originally been the name of a Frankish blacksmith. Thereafter, given the long period of their production, it became a trademark of sorts. However, Anne Stalsberg (2008, 23) does not believe that Ulfberht was a blacksmith and argues on the basis of his apparent literacy and use of crosses that he was more likely a cleric.

Archaeologists have chemically analyzed the blades of these swords and discovered that they contain a much higher carbon content than common medieval swords, resulting in much stronger, more flexible blades that would have been more durable and superior in battle. The raw material for these blades must have been crucible steel, which was not produced in Europe during this time but rather had to be imported from the East. According to 11th-century Persian scholar al-Biruni, crucible steel was produced in the area around the city of Herat (in modern-day Afghanistan) and then traded through Persia (modern-day Iran) to the West (Williams 2012, 120–121). Such far-traveled raw material was expensive and required a blacksmith's special knowledge to properly craft into a blade. Since Ulfberht swords were high-quality weapons and would have commanded higher prices than common swords, there was apparently also a trade in counterfeit Ulfberht swords. Swords with variants of the +VLFBERH+T inscription, ranging from +VLFBERHT+ (with the second cross after instead of before the T) to various versions with missing or differing letters to textlike marks have been discovered, which contain less carbon than the authentic Ulfberht swords. Clearly, it was prestigious to own such a fine sword, and the distribution in northern Europe, especially the high concentration in Scandinavia, demonstrates that at least a few wealthy Scandinavians during the Viking Age possessed some of the highest-quality weapons available in Europe at the time.

The Viking repertoire of war equipment was thus varied and, in some cases, very sophisticated. Although many of the lower-status warriors would have been able to afford only basic weapons, higher-status and elite warriors possessed costly, high-quality equipment. It seems reasonable to conclude that the weapons used by the Vikings were not any less crude or primitive than the weapons used elsewhere in Europe during the Viking Age. Considering the fact that the greatest concentration of high-quality Ulfberht swords have been discovered in Scandinavia, it could indeed be argued that the Vikings' weapons were of a superior quality.

PRIMARY DOCUMENTS

THE SAGA OF THE VOLSUNGS (LATE 13TH CENTURY)

Vǫlsunga saga (the Saga of the Volsungs) is the Old Norse-Icelandic saga relating the story of Sigurd the Dragon-Slayer. In this excerpt, Sigurd has the dwarf Regin reforge the broken sword of his father and tests its quality. He does it first by striking it against the anvil and then floating a piece of wool in a river. When, after throwing the sword into the river, the wool is cut in two as it drifts against the blade, he is satisfied. Before reforging the sword, Sigurd tests and breaks two lesser swords. The excerpt supports the notion that the Vikings were discerning about the quality of their weapons.

So Regin makes a sword, and gives it into Sigurd's hands. He took the sword, and said–

"Behold thy smithying, Regin!" and therewith smote it into the anvil, and the sword brake; so he cast down the brand, and bade him forge a better.

Then Regin forged another sword, and brought it to Sigurd, who looked thereon.

Then said Regin, "Belike thou art well content therewith, hard master though thou be in smithying."

So Sigurd proved the sword, and brake it even as the first; then he said to Regin–

"Ah, art thou, mayhappen, a traitor and a liar like to those former kin of thine?"

Therewith he went to his mother, and she welcomed him in seemly wise, and they talked and drank together.

Then spake Sigurd, "Have I heard aright, that King Sigmund gave thee the good sword Gram in two pieces?"

"True enough," she said.

So Sigurd said, "Deliver them into my hands, for I would have them."

She said he looked like to win great game, and gave him the sword. Therewith went to Sigurd to Regin, and bade him make a good sword thereof as he best might; Regin grew wroth thereat, but went into the smithy with the pieces of the sword, thinking well meanwhile that Sigurd pushed his head far enow into the matter of smithying. So he made a sword, and as he bore it forth from the forge, it seemed to the smiths as though fire burned along the edges thereof. Now he bade Sigurd take the sword, and said he knew not how to make a sword if this one failed. Then Sigurd smote it into the anvil, and cleft it down to the stock thereof, and neither burst the sword nor brake it. Then he praised the sword much, and thereafter went to the river with a lock of wool, and threw it up against the stream, and it fell asunder when it met the sword. Then was Sigurd glad, and went home.

Source: Magnusson, Eiríkr, and William Morris, trans. 1888. *Völsunga Saga: The Story of the Volsungs and Niblungs, with Certain Songs from the Elder Edda*. London: Walter Scott. 50–51.

THE SAGA OF EGILL SKALLA-GRÍMSSON (13TH CENTURY)

This excerpt is from the Old Norse-Icelandic Egils saga Skalla-Grímssonar *(the* Saga of Egil Skalla-Grimsson*) composed in the 13th century. It details*

King Erik Bloodaxe's gift of an axe to Skalla-Grim. Although the axe at first appears to be prestigious and costly, it turns out to not be of the quality that Skalla-Grim expects. This offends him, and he then recites a stanza of skaldic poetry, expressing his anger and feeling of betrayal. Skalla-Grim's disappointment reflects the high standards the Norse had for their weapons.

Thorolf Skallagrim's son made him ready one summer for a trading voyage; he purposed what he also performed, to go to Iceland and see his father. He had now been long abroad. By this he had got great store of wealth and many costly things. When ready for the voyage, he went to king Eric. And at their parting the king delivered to Thorolf an axe, which he said he wished to give to Skallagrim. The axe was snag-horned, large, gold-mounted, the hilt overlaid with silver; it was most valuable and costly.

Thorolf went his way as soon as he was ready, and his voyage sped well; he came with his ship into Borgar-firth, and at once hastened home to his father. A right joyful meeting was theirs. Then Skallagrim went down to Thorolf's ship, and had it drawn up, and Thorolf went home to Borg with twelve men. But when he came home, he gave Skallagrim King Eric's greeting, and delivered to him the axe which the king had sent him. Skallagrim took the axe and held it up, looked at it awhile, but said nothing. He fixed it up by his seat.

It chanced one day in the autumn at Borg that Skallagrim had several oxen driven home which he meant to slaughter. Two of these he had led under the house-wall, and placed with heads crossing. He took a large flat stone, and pushed it under their necks. Then he went near with the axe—the king's gift—and hewed at the oxen both at once, so that he took off the heads of the two. But the axe smote down on the stone, so that the mouth broke, and was rent through all the tempered steel. Skallagrim looked at the edge, said nothing, but went into the fire-hall, and, mounting to the wall-beam, thrust the axe up among the rafters above the door. There it lay in the smoke all the winter.

But in the spring Thorolf declared that he meant to go abroad that summer.

Skallagrim forbade him, saying: "Tis good to drive home with your wain whole. You have,' said he, 'gotten great honour by travel; but there is the old saw, "Many farings, many fortunes." Take you now here as much share of the property as you think will make you a great man.'

Thorolf said he would make yet one journey more. 'And I have,' said he, 'an urgent errand for the journey. But when I come back next time I shall settle here. But Asgerdr, your foster-child, shall go out with me to her father. This he bade me when I came west.'

Skallagrim said Thorolf would have his way.

Thereafter Thorolf went to his ship, and put it in order. And when all was ready they moved the ship out to Digra-ness, and it lay there waiting a wind. Then Asgerdr went to the ship with him. But before Thorolf left Borg Skallagrim went and took down from the rafters over the door the axe, the king's gift—and came out with it. The haft was now black with smoke, and the blade rusted. Skallagrim looked at the axe's edge. Then he handed it to Thorolf, reciting this stave:

'The fierce would-wolf's tooth-edge
Hath flaws not a few,
An axe all deceitful,
A wood cleaver weak.
Begone! worthless weapon,
With shaft smoke-begrimed:
A prince ill-beseemed it
Such present to send.'

Source: Green, Rev. William Charles, trans. 1893. *The Story of Egil Skallagrimsson: Being an Icelandic Family History of the Ninth and Tenth Centuries*, translated from Icelandic by Rev. W. C. Green. London: E. Stock. 66–67.

Further Reading

Kunz, Keneva. 1997. "The Saga of the People of Laxardal." In *The Complete Sagas of Icelanders Including 49 Tales*, edited by Viðar Hreinsson, 5 vols. Volume 5. Reykjavik: Leifur Eiríksson. 1–77.

Larrington, Carolyne, trans. 1996. *The Poetic Edda*. Oxford: Oxford University Press.

Lindsay, Thomas. 1965. "Viking Weapons." *Scottish Art Review* 10: 25–30.

Line, Philip. 2015. *The Vikings and Their Enemies: Warfare in Northern Europe*. New York: Skyhorse Publishing.

Orkisz, Jan H. 2016. "Pole-Weapons in the Sagas of the Icelanders: A Comparison of Literary and Archaeological Sources." *Acta Periodica Duellatorum, Scholarly Volume, Articles* 4(1): 177–212.

Pedersen, Anne. 2008. "Viking Weaponry." In *The Viking World*, edited by Stefan Brink with Neil Price. New York: Routledge. 204–221.

Skeat, Walter W., trans. 1900. "Passion of Saint Edmund." In *Aelfric's Lives of Saints*. The Early English Text Society, 76, 82, 94, 114, Volume 2. 314–335.

Stalsberg, Anne. 2008. "The Vlfberht Sword Blades Reevaluated." *Zeitschrift für Archäologie des Mittelalters* 36: 89–118.

Swanton, Michal, trans. 2000. *The Anglo-Saxon Chronicles*. London: Phoenix Press.

8

Vikings Were Unhygienic

What People Think Happened

This is part of a verse quoted from the songbook of the Wychwood Warriors, an Oxford University historical reenactment society seeking to recreate life and warfare in what the society refers to as "Dark Age Wessex." (Wychwood Warriors Wiki 2016). The Oxford society clearly assumes that the Vikings were unclean.

> We just fight for booze and crumpet,
> Filthy Vikings all are we!

It is difficult to know when, where, and how the notion of filthy Vikings originated, but considering living conditions in the Viking Age, the Scandinavians' idea about personal hygiene and cleanliness at that time were clearly different from today's standards. The Vikings often spent days and weeks on crowded longships, and under those conditions, it would have been difficult for them to bathe, wash clothes, and shave. In their homes in Scandinavia, those Vikings who were farmers typically lived in a longhouse, where certainly in the beginning of the Viking Age, the entire household slept in the same room and where only a partition created a division between humans and domestic animals, which attract fleas, lice, and rats. Paul C. Buckland (2000, 150) notes that human fleas are recorded from York (England), Dublin (Ireland), and the Norse settlements in Greenland. Both Else Roesdahl and Buckland draw attention also to human parasites. Roesdahl (1987, 34 and plate 5) mentions archaeological research in York, where the egg of a human intestinal parasite was found at the site. Buckland (2000) believes that human parasites were, in fact, quite common but notes that "one sample from a room in postmedieval Reykholt in Iceland, with more than a hundred *Pediculus humanus* and one crab louse, *Pthirus pubis* . . . , is clearly the residue from delousing, once a popular pastime" (150). However, such living conditions were surely the norm elsewhere in Europe during that time as well and even long after.

How the Story Became Popular

In the early 920s, the Arab Ibn Fadlān was sent out as secretary of an embassy from the caliph of Baghdad to the king of the Bulghars of the Middle Volga in Russia. There, in the encampment of the Bulghars, a Turkic-speaking people, he met a group of Swedish Vikings, the so-called Rus, who were probably a group of traders. In their encampment, he was eyewitness to the ship burial cremation of one of the Viking chieftains and the concomitant sacrifice of one of the chieftain's slave girls. In this connection, he also received secondhand information about their appearance and hygiene. He was impressed with the former but not the latter. In fact, he described them thus:

> They are the filthiest of God's creatures. They do not clean themselves after urinating or defecating, nor do they wash after having sex. They do not wash their hands after meals. They are like wandering asses . . . Every day without fail they wash their faces and their heads with the dirtiest and filthiest water there could be . . . He washes and disentangles his hair, using a comb, there in the basin, then he blows his nose and spits and does every filthy thing imaginable in the water. (Ibn Fadlān, 2012)

It is difficult to assess Fadlān's influence with regard to the idea that the Vikings were unhygienic, but certainly the media and especially the movie industry has done much to promote the idea of Vikings as filthy. For example, reference may be made to the 1958 movie *The Vikings*, directed by Richard Fleischer, which was based on the novel *The Viking* by Edison Marschall (1894–1967), an American short story writer and novelist. Aside from the plot of the movie, which takes rather a lot of liberties with regard to historical facts, it comes across as authentic in a number of ways. Among other things, it is to be lauded for the fact that neither horned helmets nor drinking out of skulls is in evidence (see chapters 9 and 11). It is questionable, however, if Kirk Douglas, who produced the movie and also stars in it, should appear as ungroomed as he sometimes does. However, the movie greatly influenced popular views of the Vikings.

What Really Happened

Everything is relative, even cleanliness. While it is likely that those Vikings who showed up on foreign shores looked rather unkempt, it is now generally believed that at least in their homes in Scandinavia or in their colonies abroad, the Vikings paid quite a bit of attention to their appearance. The name for Saturday in Old Norse-Icelandic is *laugardagr* (bath day), which suggests that people in medieval Scandinavia took a bath at least once a week.

Several Old Norse-Icelandic literary works make reference to cleanliness. The oldest of these is likely the poem *Hávamál* (*Sayings of the High One* [=Odin]). Foreign sources, too, suggest that Scandinavians in the Viking Age paid attention to cleanliness and appearance. Ibrāhīm ibn Y'a'qūb al-Turtushi, a Jewish merchant from Tortosa, Spain, who in 965 traveled to Schleswig in what is now Germany, wrote that the inhabitants of the town fabricated and used artificial eye makeup: "Both men and women use a kind of indelible cosmetic to enhance the beauty of their eyes" (Ibn Fadlān 2012, 163). Johannes Brøndsted (1965) draws attention to the fact that "[t]he Danes in England appear to have been . . . careful of their toilet, according to a literary source which says that they combed their hair, had a bath on Saturdays, and changed their linen frequently 'in order the more easily to overcome the chastity of women and procure the daughters of noblemen as their mistresses'" (254). It is unknown if the Scandinavians had any kind of real soap. Brøndsted (1965, 254) commented that for washing coarser clothes, they probably used cow urine, which contains ammonia, a cleansing element.

In addition, the Sagas of Icelanders make reference to saunas and hot baths in Norway and Iceland. The Icelanders soon learned to take advantage of geothermal hot water, and *Eyrbyggja saga* (the *Saga of the People of Eyrr*) provides a detailed description of a sauna: approximately half of it was dug into the ground, and it had a hole in the top for pouring water onto the stove by people outside. Finally, the Sagas of Icelanders mention laundry, which was done in streams sometimes distant from the farmhouse, as one of the many tasks of women (Jochens 1995, 123). Hair-washing is referred to as well. Jenny Jochens (1995) maintains that "[w]ashing of hair was located at the interstices between laundering and bathing, work and pleasure, indoors and outdoors. In the saga world it was performed only by women for men, children and themselves individually, but not for other women, if we trust the silence of the narratives on this point" (125).

Finally, there is ample evidence from archaeological finds that the Vikings were concerned about their personal appearance. Several toilet implements have been found, such as ear spoons (to remove earwax), combs of antler and bone (to groom head and facial hair—and potentially get rid of lice), and washing bowls. Other items have been interpreted as tweezers and toothpicks. For illustrations of combs and an ear spoon, see Haraldr Ólafsson (2000, 150–151).

It is noteworthy that people in Scandinavia and Iceland during the Viking Age took precautions against diseases that could easily be transmitted due to unsanitary living conditions. Two of the Sagas of Icelanders tell of epidemics. One is *Eiríks saga rauða* (the *Saga of Eric the Red*), which relates that on a farm in Norse Greenland, there was an epidemic that almost wiped out the entire household. The other is *Eyrbyggja saga* (the *Saga of the People of Eyrr*), in which it is told that a disease was brought to the farm Froda in Iceland by a visitor from the Hebrides. This visitor was the first to die, and in the saga, the spread of the disease is attributed to the neglect of the mistress of the house to burn the deceased person's bedclothes and bedstraws.

PRIMARY DOCUMENTS

SAYINGS OF THE HIGH ONE (1270)

Hávamál (Sayings of the High One [= Odin]) is an Old Norse-Icelandic eddic poem. It is preserved in the Codex Regius *from around 1270. It is not a unified poem; in fact, it is believed that the stanzas are drawn together from at least six sequences by a compiler, who clearly conceived of them as having been uttered by Odin. The first part of the poem (stanzas 1–77), often referred to as the guest's section, is the most famous. The stanzas tell rather cynically about rules of conduct in the Viking Age. The dating of the poem has been disputed, but the general view is that at least sections of the poem must date to the beginning of the Viking Age. In stanzas 4 and 61, the poet emphasizes cleanliness:*

4. He who comes for a meal requires water, a towel and a hearty welcome—a word of good cheer if he can get it, and polite attention.

61. A man should wash himself and take a meal before riding to court, even if he is not too well clad. No man should be ashamed of his shoes or trousers or of his horse either, though he had not a good one.

Source: Clarke, E. Martin. 1923. *The Hávamál with Selections from Other Poems of The Edda, Illustrating the Wisdom of the North in Heathen Times.* Cambridge: Cambridge University Press. 45, 59.

THE SAGA OF THE PEOPLE OF EYRR (13TH CENTURY)

Eyrbyggja saga (*the* Saga of the People of Eyrr) *was likely composed in the middle of the 13th century. It tells the story of the people living on the northern shores of the Snæfellsnes Peninsula on the west coast of Iceland. The saga provides a description of a sauna. The context of the description is that the farmer or landowner Styr (referred to as Stir in the translation) hired two troublesome warriors, Halli and Leiknir, both berserkers (referred to bareserks in the translation). The former berserker demands Styr's daughter in marriage, and, as a last resort to prevent the marriage, Styr uses his sauna to kill the berserks.*

Now that happed to tell of next which is aforewritten, that the Bareserks were with Stir, and when they had been there awhile, Halli fell to talking with Asdis, Stir's daughter. She was a young woman and a stately, proud of attire, and somewhat high-minded; but when Stir knew of their talk together, he bade Halli not to do him that shame and heartburn in beguiling his daughter.

Halli answered: "No shame it is to thee though I talk with thy daughter, nor will I do that to thy dishonour; but I will tell thee straightly that I have so much love in my heart for her, that I know not how to put it out of my mind. And now," said Halli, "will I seek for fast friendship with thee, and pray thee to give me thy daughter Asdis, and thereto in return will I put my friendship and true service, and so much strength through the power of my brother Leikner, that there shall not be in Iceland so much glory from two men's services as we two shall give thee; and our furtherance shall strengthen thy chieftainship more than if thou gavest thy daughter to the mightiest bonder of Broadfirth, and that shall be in return for our not being strong of purse. But if thou wilt not do for me my desire, that shall cut our friendship atwain; and then each must do as he will in his own matter; and little avail will it be to thee then to grumble about my talk with Asdis."

When he had thus spoken, Stir was silent, and thought it somewhat hard to answer, but he said in a while:

"Whether is this spoken with all thine heart, or is it a vain word, and seekest thou a quarrel?"

"So shalt thou answer," said Halli, "as if mine were no foolish word; and all our friendship lies on what thine answer will be in this matter."

Stir answered: "Then will I talk the thing over with my friends, and take counsel with them how I shall answer this."

Said Halli: "The matter shalt thou talk over with whomsoever pleases thee within three nights, but I will not that this answer to me drag on longer than that, because I will not be a dangler over this betrothal."

And therewithal they parted.

The next morning Stir rode east to Holyfell, and when he came there, Snorri bade him abide; but Stir said that he would talk with him, and then ride away.

Snorri asked if he had some troublous matter on hand to talk of. "So it seems to me," said Stir.

Snorri said: "Then we will go up on to the Holy Fell, (1) for those redes have been the last to come to nought that have been taken there."

"Therein thou shalt have thy will," said Stir.

So they went upon to the mount, and there sat talking all day till evening, nor did any man know what they said together; and then Stir rode home.

But the next morning Stir and Halli went to talk together, and Halli asked Stir how his case stood.

Stir answered: "It is the talk of men that thou seemest somewhat bare of money, so what wilt thou do for this, since thou hast no fee to lay down therefor?"

Halli answered: "I will do what I may, since money fails me."

Says Stir: "I see that it will mislike thee if I give thee not my daughter; so now will I do as men of old, and will let thee do some great deed for this bridal."

"What is it, then?" said Halli.

"Thou shalt break up," says Stir, "a road through the lava out to Bearhaven, and raise a boundary-wall over the lava betwixt our lands, and make a burg (2) here at the head of the lava; and when this work is done, I will give thee Asdis my daughter."

Halli answered: "I am not wont to work, yet will I say yea to this, if thereby I may the easier have the maiden for wife."

Stir said that this then should be their bargain.

Thereafter they began to make the road, and the greatest of man's-work it is; (3) and they raised the wall whereof there are still tokens, and thereafter wrought the burg. But while they were at the work, Stir let build a hot bath at his house at Lava, and it was dug down in the ground, and there was a window over the furnace, so that it might be fed from without, and wondrous hot was that place.

Now when either work was nigh finished, on the last day whereon Halli and his brother were at work on the burg, it befell that thereby passed Asdis,

Stir's daughter, and close to the homestead it was. Now she had done on her best attire, and when Halli and his brother spake to her, she answered nought.

Then sang Halli this stave:

O fair-foot, O linen-girt goddess that beareth
The flame that is hanging from fair limbs adown!
Whither now hast thou dight thee thy ways to be wending,
O fair wight, O tell me, and lie not in telling?
For all through the winter, O wise-hearted warden
Of the board of the chess-play, not once I beheld thee
From out of the houses fare this-wise afoot,
So goodly of garments, so grand of array.

Then Leikner sang:

The ground of the gold-sun that gleams in the isle-belt
But seldom hath dight her the headgear so stately.
The fir of the fire of the perch of the falcon
Is laden with load of fine work of the loom.
O ground strewn with jewels, O fair-spoken goddess
Of beakers the bright, now I bid thee be telling
What is it that under thy pride lieth lurking?
What hast thou thereunder of more than we wot?

Therewith they parted. The Bareserks went home in the evening and were much foredone, as is wont to be the way of those men who are skin-changers, that they become void of might when the Bareserk fury falls from them. Stir went to meet them, and thanked them for their work, and bade them come to the bath and rest thereafter, and so they did.

But when they were come into the bath. Stir let the bath-chamber be closed, and had stones laid on the trap-door which was over the fore-chamber, and spread a raw and slimy neat's-hide down by the top entrance thereof; and then he let feed the furnace from without through that window which was thereover.

Then waxed the bath so hot that the Bareserks might not abide it, and leaped up at the door, and Halli brake open the trap-door and got out, but fell on the hide, and Stir gave him his death-blow; but when Leikner would have sprung out by the opening, Stir thrust him through and he fell back into the bath, and died there. Then Stir let lay out the corpses, and they were carried out into the lava, and were cast into that dale which is in the lava, and is so deep that one can see nought therefrom but the heavens above it, and that is beside that self-same road.

Now over the burial of the Bareserks Stir sang this stave:

Methought that the raisers of riot of spear-mote
Would nowise and never be meek and mild-hearted.
Or hearken the bidding of them that are hardening
The onrush of Ali's high wind and hard weather.
No dread have I now of their dealings against me,
Of the masterful bearing of the lads of the battle;
For now I, the slayer of tarrying, truly,
With my brand have marked out a meet place for the Bareserks.

But when Snorri the Priest knew these things he rode out to under Lava, and the twain Snorri and Stir sat again together all day, and this got abroad of their talk, that Stir had betrothed Asdis his daughter to Snorri the Priest, and the wedding was to be held the next autumn; and it was the talk of men that both of these two might be deemed to have waxed from these haps, and this alliance. For Snorri was the better counselled and the wiser man, but Stir the more adventurous and pushing; but either had strong kinship and great following about the countryside.

Source: Morris, William, and Eiríkr Magnússon, trans. 1892. *The Story of the Ere-Dwellers (Eyrbyggja Saga) with the Story of the Heath-Slayings (Heiðarvíga saga) as Appendix*. London: Bernard Quaritch. 66–71.

Further Reading

Brøndsted, Johannes. 1965. *The Vikings*, translated by Kalle Skov. London: Penguin.

Buckland, Carl C. 2000. "The North Atlantic Environment." In *Vikings: The North Atlantic Saga*, edited by William W. Fitzhugh and Elisabeth I. Ward. Washington: Smithsonian Institution Press. 146–153.

Ibn Fadlān. 2012. *Ibn Fadlān and the Land of Darkness: Arab Travellers in the Far North,* translated with an Introduction by Paul Lunde and Caroline Stone. London: Penguin. 45–47.

Jochens, Jenny. 1995. *Women in Old Norse Society*. Ithaca: Cornell University Press.

Ólafsson, Haraldur. 2000. "Sagas of Western Expansion." In *Vikings: The North Atlantic Saga*, edited by William W. Fitzhugh and Elizabeth I. Ward. Washington: Smithsonian Institution Press. 146–153.

Roesdahl, Else. 1991. *The Vikings*, translated by Susan M. Margeson and Kirsten Williams. London: Penguin Press.

Wychwood Warriors Wiki. 2016. "Songbook: Filthy Vikings (All Are We)." Accessed September 20, 2017. http://wychwood.wikidot.com/songbook-filth995.

9

Vikings Wore Horned Helmets

What People Think Happened

Anyone acquainted with souvenir stores in Scandinavia or Iceland will have seen a Viking with a horned helmet—be it a shaving-cream brush, an egg timer, a miniature Viking figure, or a life-size plastic helmet with horns and sometimes blond pigtails. It's hard to come across a Viking who doesn't wear a horned helmet.

For a long time, the horned helmet has also made its appearance in paintings, children's books, and advertisements. Roberta Frank (2000, 200) draws attention to the fact that as early as July 23, 1895, a horn-helmeted Viking appeared on a Scandinavian Cruise Line menu of the Hamburg-America liner *Columbia*. Admittedly, the classic cow-horn helmet has sometimes had to compete with helmets furnished with other kinds of protuberances, especially wings. Frank (2000) notes that "[t]he pagan vikings besieging Paris in nineteenth-century French art remained elegantly winged throughout their ordeal" (200). However, the horned version of the helmet is the one that has endured.

In the United States, the Minnesota Vikings wear helmets with painted horns. Although many practices and customs have changed since the football team first began play during the 1961 season, one thing has never changed: the team's horned helmets. From Fran Tarkenton in 1961 to Everson Griffen in 2016, each and every player has worn the horned helmet. The image of the horned Viking is so popular that some fans attend games in Viking regalia, and the team's mascot, Viktor the Viking, is generally furnished with a horned helmet. The mascot is so sought after in the Midwest that in 2017, he could demand an hourly salary of $325 for showing up at events, such as the opening of a business or a wedding. When in 1991 Ernest Beck, a staff reporter for *The Wall Street Journal*, questioned Bob Hagan, spokesman for the Minnesota Vikings football team, about the horns on Viktor the Viking's helmet, Hagan's response was: "We believe Vikings did wear horned helmets."

Beck comments that "Mr. Hagan hadn't heard that academics want to recast Vikings as warm and fuzzy, but he doesn't think the team would ever alter its mascot. Still, he takes a balanced view, 'Vikings were fighters, but they weren't bad people,' he says, noting that the team chose the mascot because many Scandinavians settled in Minnesota. 'We wouldn't name our team after bad people.'"

The beloved Hagar the Horrible, the main character of the eponymous comic strip created in 1973 by Dik Browne, also wears a horned helmet and continues to do so even after Browne's sons took over the comic strip after their father's death. Finally, all the male Vikings are furnished with horned helmets in the animated TV series *Vicky the Viking*, based on *Vicke Viking* by Swedish author Runer Johnson, who won the German Children's Book Award for the book in 1965 (see chapter 3).

How the Story Became Popular

There is general consensus that Swedish artist Gustav Malmström was the first to provide Vikings with horned helmets and that he did so in illustrations made in the 1820s for the writer, professor, and bishop Esaias Tegnér (1782–1846), who in 1825 published his national romantic epos *Frithiofs saga* (the *Saga of Frithiof*), a poem based on a mythical heroic saga composed in Iceland in the late 13th or early 14th century (see chapter 1). The poem became very popular and caused him to be considered the father of modern poetry in Sweden. Presumably Malmström got the idea of a horned helmet from ancient archaeological finds. Deities depicted with horns or antlers are found in many different regions of the world. However, it is also possible that he was inspired by the fantastical headgear that in the late Middle Ages became popular among knights in particular for tournaments. It seems unlikely that Malmström used Scandinavian sources, because in Scandinavia, horned helmets, which date from the Bronze Age, were not found until after his death. There is a remote possibility that he was inspired by the four helmet-plate patrices made of bronze from Björnhovda in the parish of Torslunda on the island of Öland, Sweden, which were found in 1870. The four dies illustrate what is probably the pagan god Odin along with his two ravens, Huginn (thought) and Muninn (memory), which are typically described as perching on his shoulders, and date from the Vendel era, which precedes the Viking Age. It is very unlikely that he was inspired by images of Satan in order to make Vikings look even more barbarian and pagan.

The person credited with the idea of popularizing the horned helmet is Carl Emil Doepler (1824–1905), a costume designer who in 1876 created horned helmets for the first Bayreuth Festival production of Richard Wagner's famous opera, *Ring des Nibelungen* (the *Ring of the Nibelungs*), even though the opera was set in Germany and not Scandinavia (see chapter 1). The same designer also added horns and even feathers to helmets in his illustrations to *Nordisch-Germanische Götter und Helden: Unsere Vorzeit* (*Nordic-Germanic Gods and Heroes: Our Past*) by Wilhelm Wagner and Jakob Nover, which was published in 1882. With Carl Emil Doepler's costume designs and illustrations, the stereotype of a horned Viking was born.

During the 1890s, more horn-helmeted Vikings appeared regularly in books for children and young adults. Frank (2000, 201) draws attention, for example, to the ninth edition of R. M. Ballentyne's *Erling the Bold: A Tale of the Norse Sea Kings* (1890) and M. Zeno Diemer's illustrations to Sabine Baring-Gould's *Grettir the Outlaw: A Story of Iceland* (1890). What this meant is that the generation of young people at the turn of the twentieth century were imprinted with the image of the Vikings as horn-helmeted.

History books of a popular nature also appropriated the horned helmet for their Vikings, especially books published in Germany and England. Frank (2000) mentions as an example the fact that "[a] 1904 drawing of the Eddic hero Helgi, his perfect horned helmet, and his blonde valkyrie, appeared in the much-altered sixth edition of Johannes Scherr's *Germania*," and comments that "[t]he five previous editions have no horned helmets" (202).

Scandinavians showed somewhat more restraint in their use of the horned helmet. If in their books the illustrators placed this kind of headgear on a character, they reserved it for gods, giants, and legendary heroes. Frank (2000, 203) mentions as an example Frederik Winkel Horn's 1898 two-volume translation of Saxo Grammaticus's *Gesta Danorum* (Deeds of the Danes). She notes that there are around 300 illustrations by Louis Moe in the two volumes, but that in the first volume, the horned helmet appears only on a god, a giant, a Saxon, a Slavic barbarian, and a mythical king, whereas in the second volume, which is concerned primarily with the Viking Age, no horned helmets can be detected.

Even though the Viking warriors wore conical helmets without horns in the illustrations of Gustav Storm's *Snorre Sturlasons Kongesagaer*, a Norwegian translation of Snorri Sturluson's early-13th-century *Heimskringla (Disc of the World)*, which was published in Christiania (Oslo) in 1899, there is little evidence that the existence of the horned helmet was questioned.

PRIMARY DOCUMENT
ESAIAS TEGNÉR'S *FRITHIOFS SAGA* (1825)

In 1820, Esaias Tegnér published portions of the epic Frithiofs saga *in Iduna. Five more cantos were published in 1822, and in 1825, the entire poem was published. The poem was illustrated by Gustav Malmström, who depicted the Vikings with horned helmets. The book, which was translated into several languages, made Tegnér famous throughout Europe and caused him to transfer from his study in Lund to the bishop's seat in Växjö. Horned helmets also appeared in new illustrations in later versions, such as the 1912 retelling* Song of Frithiof *by George Cantrell Allen, illustrated by Thomas Heath Robinson (1869–1954).*

Source: Allen, George Cantrell. 1912. *The Song of Frithiof*. London: Henry Frowde; Hodder and Stoughton. 15.

THE HORNED HELMET AND THE WINGED HELMET (1905–1908)

In her 2000 article "The Invention of the Viking Horned Helmet," published in International Scandinavian and Medieval Studies in Memory of Gerd Wolfgang Weber, *edited by Michael Dallapiazza, Olaf Hansen, Preben Meulengracht Sørensen, and Yvonne S. Bonnetain (Trieste: Edizioni Parnaso, 2000), Roberta Frank mentions that a letter was sent to the Saga-Book of the Viking Club in 1905 about the veracity of the winged helmet. Karl Blind (1826–1907), a German writer on politics, history, and mythology, who found refuge in England for his revolutionary activities in 1852, responded to the letter in the "Viking Notes" of the issue. He answered in the negative but commented that the horned helmet was worn by the Thraciens, and that they were related to the Norsemen and the Germanic race. Frank also mentions that in* Saga-Book *its district secretary, Charles Watts Whistler (1856–1913), a writer of historical fiction based on archaeological discoveries and Old English and Old Norse-Icelandic literary works, reiterated a year or two later that there was no evidence for the winged helmet, but that there was plenty of evidence for the horned helmet.*

REPORTED FIND OF A VIKING HELMET IN IRELAND.

In describing to the Irish Royal Society of Antiquaries in June, 1905, the find of a Danish gold pin at Clontarf, Mr. Milligan also mentioned that in 1903 he found in Ards peninsula a splendid bronze brooch of the Viking period, with a Viking helmet. Unfortunately the material of which the latter is made was not mentioned in the brief report of the meeting given in the "Antiquary," but in any case the find is worth recording, helmets being extremely rare. Even the Museum of Christiania does not contain a single perfect specimen, though fragments are not infrequent. Of one thing we may be certain, that it was not provided with the wings so dear to the artists who illustrate Viking stories.

THE WINGED HELMET MYTH.

Against those anachronisms, probably evolved from some late German source of the "Lohengrin" order, I, as a sufferer, would hereby register a solemn protest, being absolutely unable to find any authority for them, though for the horned helm, and also for the boar-crested helm, there is plenty, examples of both being in the British Museum, besides the well-known early pictured representations of the former, and Beowulf mentions of the latter.

......

In reply to an enquiry as to whether he knows any authority for the winged helmet, which is the conventional head gear of a Viking chief in romances and on the stage, Dr. Karl Blind writes:-

I can only say that I do not know of any winged helmet having probably been worn by Vikings. So far as there are any representations, they had caps, or morions, without such adornment. Historically we find from Herodotos that one of the Thrakian tribes in the army of Xerxes had brazen helmets, with the ears and horns of an ox in brass, and above them, crests. The Thrakians were kindred to the Germanic race; more specially to the Norsemen, partly also to what would now be called Teutons.

In Plutarch ("Caius Marius"), the Kimbirans,—whom he describes (as Tacitus does the Germans) as of tall stature, and blue-eyed, and whose name he derives from the German language,—are said to have worn helmets with the head and open jaws of frightful wild beasts, above which *high plumes* were fixed. They wore white shields. (Odin wore a white shield.)

The Kimbrians came from what is now Schleswig-Holstein and Jutland. Of German tribes, the Herulians apparently came originally from Scandinavia, migrating as far as what is now Bavaria in Germany, and even to Asia Minor. The winged, white-plumed helmet may, therefore, have been used, in ancient times, also in Scandinavia; the Kimbrians, of yore, dwelling midway between Scandinavia and Germany, and wearing, as shown, those helm ornaments.

Odin-Wodan, in his quality of God of Battles, wore a helmet. In modern sculpture, at least, wings are added to it, which fits him well as the all-pervading World-Wanderer and Stormy Leader of the nocturnal Wild-Chace. Probably, Wing-Thor also means the Winged God of Thunder.

In the Eddic "Lay of Alvis" he says of himself:
Wing-Thor I am hight;
Wide I have wandered—

and according to this idea, he might have got the wing attribute represented in his helmet, like Hermes, the much-travelling God, in his cap and shoes.

Source: Whistler, C. W., "Reported Find of a Viking Helmet in Ireland," "The Winged Helmet Myth." *Saga-Book* 5(1907–1908): 51; Hon, The. "Viking Notes." *Saga-Book* 4(1905–1906): 412.

What Really Happened

No Viking Age horned helmet has been discovered in Scandinavia. In fact, very few helmets from the Viking Age have been found. The best-known Viking helmet that can be attributed to Viking armor was found in 1943 in a burial mound near Gjermundbu in Ringerike, Norway, along with other Viking Age artifacts, such as tools, swords, and chain mail. This 10th-century helmet was found in separate fragments, which make up only one-third or a quarter of the helmet. Reconstruction of the helmet shows that it consisted of a framework in the form of a horizontal rim and two vertical metal straps. One of the straps extends from the back of the head to the forehead, whereas the other extends from one ear to the other. Four plates are attached to this framework with rivets in order to fashion a skull-piece. The ocularia, which protect the face and the nose, are also fastened to the horizontal rim.

Another famous Viking helmet is the Tjele helmet, which has been dated to the latter half of the 10th century. It was discovered near the village Tjele in Jutland, Denmark, in 1850 along with hammers, anvils, tongs, and other things belonging to a blacksmith. The helmet, which was originally thought to be parts of a saddle mount, has been identified by archaeologists as a spectacle low-domed helmet. Unfortunately, only fragments of the helmet, which are in iron and bronze, have been preserved, but recent research suggests that in its original form it was quite similar to the Gjermundbu helmet.

In addition to the Gjermundbu and Tjele helmets, two fragments of a helmet from the island of Gotland and one from Kiev have been found. These finds pretty much sum up what is known from archaeology about helmets in the Viking Age. None of these show signs of horns, wings, feathers, knobs, or the like.

For finds of Scandinavian helmets with horns, it is necessary to go back to the Nordic Bronze Age (ca. 1100 BC–ca. 900 BC). Here the most famous helmets are the so-called Viksø helmets, which were discovered in 1942 on the site of a bog near the town of Viksø on the island of Zealand in Denmark. The two helmets are made of bronze and feature two long bull-like horns. It is doubtful that the helmets were produced in Scandinavia and even more doubtful that they were used for warfare, because they are quite fragile. It is now believed that they were used for ceremonial purposes. The beautiful and well-preserved helmets discovered in the early 1880s in Vendel, a parish in the Swedish province of Uppland, and which have been dated to the Nordic Iron Age (ca. 500 BC–ca. AD 800) also have no horns.

In addition, Old Norse-Icelandic literature makes no reference to horns on a helmet. In fact, helmets may well have been rare among Vikings. Iron was expensive, and it is likely that very few warriors could afford helmets (Foote and Wilson 1980, 279). Also, horned helmets would have been impractical for warriors. The horns, which serve no practical function, would have been inconvenient on crowded ships, and in battles on land, horned helmets could easily have gotten entangled in tree branches. Finally, helmets were used for defensive purposes and to protect against blows. A blow by a sword or an axe struck on a horn or some other protuberance would transmit the shock into the skull and cause severe brain damage.

If the Vikings wore helmets, they would probably have been conical helmets made of leather, which is degradable and would not have survived. Philip Line (2015, 36–39), who has written extensively about Viking warfare on both land and sea, analyzed the development of helmets in the Viking Age and found no traces of horns. The bottom line is that Viking Age helmets had no horns and that the horned helmet is a product of the fantasy of 19th-century artists.

PRIMARY DOCUMENT
HELMETS FROM *HEIMSKRINGLA* (CA. 1230)

Snorri Sturluson's (1178/9–1241) Heimskringla (Disc of the World) *received a lot of attention, especially in Norway, where it became known as a "second Bible." In the late 19th century, Gustav Storm translated it into Norwegian under the title* Snorre Sturlasons Kongesagaer. *The volume is copiously illustrated. The illustrators are Halfdan Egedius, Christian Krohg, Gerhard Munthe, Eilif Petersen, Erik Werenskiold, and Wilhelm Metlesen. All Vikings in these illustrations wear conical helmets. The first illustration shows King Eric's men climbing on board King Olaf Tryggvason's ship after his defeat. The second shows King Olaf Haraldsson's first Viking expedition.*

Source: Sturlason, Snorre. 1899. *Kongesagaer*, translated by Gustav Storm. Kristiania [Oslo]: J. M. Stenersen and Co.

Further Reading

Beck, Ernest. 1999. "Hagar, How Horrible! Those Vikings Simply Aren't You." *The Wall Street Journal.* January 8, 1999. A1.

Brøndsted, Johannes. 1965. *The Vikings*, translated by Kalle Skov. London: Penguin.

Foote, Peter, and David M. Wilson. 1980. *The Viking Achievement: The Society and Culture of Early Medieval Scandinavia.* London: Sidgwick & Jackson.

Frank, Roberta. 2000. "The Invention of the Viking Horned Helmet." In *International Scandinavian and Medieval Studies in Memory of Gerd Wolfgang Weber*, edited by Michael Dallapiazza, Olaf Hansen, Preben Meulengracht Sørensen, and Yvonne S. Bonnetain. Trieste: Edizioni Parnaso. 199–208.

Line, Philip. 2015. *The Vikings and Their Enemies: Warfare in Northern Europe.* New York: Skyhorse Publishing.

10

Vikings Carved the Blood Eagle

What People Think Happened

Carving the blood eagle is a bizarre and gruesome form of slaughter or sacrifice described in Old Norse-Icelandic sources. This method of killing involves forcing the living victim's ribs apart and then tearing out the lungs from the back to form the shape of an eagle's wings.

There are only two sources that provide details about this form of killing or ritual. One is *Ragnarssona þáttr* (the *Tale of Ragnar's Sons*), which is found in *Hauksbók* (*Haukr's Book*), a medieval Icelandic manuscript from the first half of the 14th century. It tells of the execution of the Northumbrian king Ella (d. 867) by the sons of Ragnar Shaggy-Breeches, a legendary Viking hero. According to legend, Ragnar was captured and tortured in a snake pit by King Ella. In order to avenge his father, Ragnar's son Ivar the Boneless captured King Ella and carved the blood eagle on Ella's back with the help of his brothers. The other is *Orkneyinga saga* (the *Saga of the Orkney Islanders*) from the end of the 12th or the beginning of the 13th century. The saga relates that Torf-Einar, earl of the Orkney Islands, had Halfdan Longleg, the son of the Norwegian king Harald Fairhair, executed by having his men slice the spine of Halfdan Longleg with a sword and then dragging out his lungs through the slits in the back. In this narrative, the ritual is associated with Odin, because it is mentioned that Torf-Einar gave Halfdan Longleg to Odin for the victory he had won. Snorri Sturluson's early-13th-century work *Heimskringla* (*Disc of the World*) contains an account of the event described in *Orkneyinga saga*, though in this work, the deed is performed by Torf-Einar himself.

In addition, there are references to the blood eagle in a Latin work, *Gesta Danorum* (*Deeds of the Danes*), by early-13th-century Danish historian Saxo Grammaticus; in *Orms þáttr Stórólfssonar* (the *Tale of Ormr Stórólfsson*), preserved in *Flateyjarbók* (the *Book of Flatey*) from the end of the 14th century, in which the victim is the giant Brusi; and in two medieval Icelandic poems. One is a skaldic poem *Knútsdrápa* (the *Lay of Knut*) composed by Sighvat Thordarson in honor of King Cnut (d. 1035) in the early 12th century, which in the first stanza relates that Ivar the Boneless killed King Ella and carved the blood eagle on his back. The other is the eddic poem *Reginsmál* (the *Lay of Regin*), the date of which has been disputed, where toward the end of the poem, the anonymous poet makes reference to the fact that Sigurd cut the blood eagle on the back of Lyngvi, the killer of his father, Sigmund.

How the Story Became Popular

It is hard to know how and when the fable about carving the blood eagle became popular, but it is a fact that the story of the carving of the blood eagle has fascinated both scholars and Viking Age enthusiasts for a long time and became more sensational as the centuries passed. As Roberta Frank (1984) points out: "The existence of different versions of the rite was noted before 1645 by the Danish scholar Stephanius in his running commentary to Saxo. By the beginning of the nineteenth century, the various saga motifs—eagle sketch, rib division, lung surgery, and 'saline stimulant'—were combined in inventive sequences designed for maximum horror" (334).

Until quite recently, scholars within the field of Old Norse literature and Scandinavian mythology believed that the blood eagle existed and was a form of human sacrifice. C. F. Keary (1891) mentions the sacrifice as a "barbarous method of execution . . . invented in the North" and comments that "[l]ike most half-savages, the Vikings knew towards their enemies no honourable code; they were as treacherous and deceitful as they were brave and cruel" (163). E. O. G. Turville-Petre (1964) referred to it as a "peculiarly revolting form of human sacrifice" and commented that "[w]hile it is plain that it was not prompted by brutality alone, the inner significance of the act remains obscure" (254–55). In addition, some scholars have, as noted by Frank (1984, 341), attempted to find support for the existence of the ritual in archaeology, on Viking Age picture stones, and in medieval literature composed outside of Scandinavia. Jan de Vries (1956, 1, 411) drew attention to a Neolithic skeleton with damage to its rib cage and shoulders, found in Heiligenthal, a village in the Mansfeld-Südharz district in Germany, and suggested that it might point to a form of slaughter similar to carving the blood eagle.

Alfred P. Smyth (1977) pointed to the image of an eagle hovering threateningly above a human being on a Viking Age stone from Stora Hammar on the island of Gotland, Sweden, and argued that the carving presents "either the sacrifice of King Vikarr [a legendary Norwegian king] or a blood-eagling ritual" (210, fn. 50). Smyth (1977) also claimed to have found "the earliest reference to the ritual of the blood-eagle" in the *Passio Sancti Eadmundi* (*Passion of Saint Edmund*) written by Abbo of Fleury in the 980s, in which the torture of Saint Edmund is described, and claims that "[t]he description is sufficiently detailed to suggest that we have here an accurate account of a body subjected to the ritual of the blood-eagle" (212–13).

The media has done much to perpetuate the blood eagle myth. In 2005, novelist Craig Russel (also known as Christopher Galt) published the novel *Blood Eagle*. The film version of the novel was produced by Tivoli Film for German public broadcaster ARD only a few years later under the title *Blutadler* (*Blood Eagle*), which premiered on November 3, 2012. The premise of the crime movie, directed by Nils Willbrand, is that two women were murdered in the same awful manner by carving the blood eagle on them. The killer challenges and derides the police via email, which suggests that the perpetrator of the crime is a serial killer living in some strange world of fantasy or delusion. As the chief police officer and his team investigate further, they are, according to the trailer of the movie, drawn into a strange and dark world of Viking myth and pagan religious cult.

In addition, on April 10, 2014, the seventh episode of the second season of the History Channel's *Vikings* and the 16th episode of the series overall was aired. This episode, also called "Blood Eagle," was written by creator Michael Hirst and directed by Kari Skogland. The episode appears to be loosely based on information culled from *Ragnarssona þáttr*, *Orkneyinga saga*, and *Gesta Danorum*, combined with quite a bit of imagination on the part of the producers. The gist of the episode concerning the blood eagle, a six-minute sequence of bloody horror, is that Ragnar carves the blood eagle on Jarl Borg, who undergoes the torture without crying out and therefore, according to the script, secures for himself a place in Valhalla, the mighty hall in Old Norse-Icelandic mythology where Odin gathers about him those slain in battle.

PRIMARY DOCUMENT

HISTORY OF THE ANGLO-SAXONS (1851)

King Ella of Northumbria succeeded to the throne in either 862 or 863 on the deposition of Osbert. According to Danish and Old Norse-Icelandic sources, King Ella was responsible for the death of Ragnar Shaggy-Breeches, a Viking leader. The Anglo-Saxon Chronicle *reports that in retaliation, the so-called Great Heathen Army, consisting mostly of Danish Vikings, invaded England a couple of years later and landed in Northumbria. King Ella and Osbert joined forces but were both slain in combat.*

The invaders, although in many bands, like the Grecian host before Troy, yet submitted to the predominance of Ingwar and Ubbo, two of the sons of Ragnar. Of these two, Ingwar was distinguished for a commanding genius, and Ubbo for his fortitude; both were highly courageous, and inordinately cruel.

In the next spring, the invaders roused from their useful repose, and marched into Yorkshire. The metropolis of the county was their first object; and, on the first of March, it yielded to their attack. Devastation followed their footsteps; they extended their divisions to the Tyne, but, without passing it, returned to York.

Osbert and Ella, having completed their pacification, moved forwards, accompanied with eight of their earls, and, on the 12th of April, assaulted the Northmen near York. The Danes, surprised by the attack, fled into the city. The English pursued with the eagerness of anticipated victory, broke down the slight walls, and entered, conflicting promiscuously with their enemies; but, having abandoned the great advantage of their superior discipline, the English rushed only to destruction. No nation could hope to excel the Northmen in personal intrepidity or manual dexterity; from their childhood they were exercised in single combat and disorderly warfare; the disunited Northumbrians were therefore cut down with irremediable slaughter. Osbert and Ella, their chiefs, and most of their army, perished. The sons of Ragnar inflicted a cruel and inhuman retaliation on Ella, for their father's sufferings. They divided his back, spread his ribs into the figure of an eagle, and agonised his lacerated flesh by the addition of the saline stimulant.

After this battle, decisive of the fate of Northumbria, it appeared no more as an Anglo-Saxon kingdom. The people beyond the Tyne appointed Egbert as their sovereign, but in a few years he was expelled, and one Ricseg took the shadowy diadem. In 876 he died with grief at the distresses of his country, and another Egbert obtained the nominal honours. But Ingwar was the Danish chief, who, profiting by his victory, assumed the sceptre of Northumbria from the Humber to the Tyne.

Source: Turner, Sharon. 1851. *The History of the Anglo-Saxons*, 4 vols. London, 1799–1805. 7th edition. Volume 4. London: Longman, Brown, Green, and Longmans. 438–440.

What Really Happened

It was not until 1984 that the story about carving the blood eagle was debunked by Frank (1984). She points out that it is on the basis of only 12 words in Sighvat Thordarson's *Knútsdrápa* that scholars have regarded the blood eagle slaughter as an authentic form of sacrifice in the Viking Age. With the exception of *Reginsmál*, the other literary witnesses are late and unreliable, and even the stanza in question in "Reginsmál" is now believed to be a late addition. It is therefore possible that the repugnant descriptions of the slaughter in the later sources are based on a misunderstanding of earlier skaldic poetry, that most difficult and intractable of all Old Norse-Icelandic genres.

Frank subjected the half stanza in *Knútsdrápa* to careful analysis. The following shows the original Old Norse text along with her literal translation:

Ok Ellu bak,	And Ella's back,
at, lét, hinn's sat,	at had the one who dwelt,
Ívarr, ara,	Ivar, with eagle,
Iorvík, skorit.	York, cut.

Earlier editors and translators of the poem have reordered the 12 words and offered translations such as "And Ivar, who dwelt at York, cut an eagle on Ella's back" or "And Ivar, who dwelt at York, had an eagle cut on Ella's back." In contrast, Frank is of the opinion that "eagle" is not the direct object of the sentence, but that it has an instrumental force. She argues in favor of translating the half stanza as follows: "And Ivar, who dwelt at York, had Ella's back cut by an eagle." The difference is only slight, but this translation permits the view that Ivar had Ella's back scored or incised with the image of an eagle or that Ivar left Ella's corpse to be lacerated by a real eagle. The latter interpretation—that Ella's corpse was left—would seem more natural, considering the many references in skaldic poetry to eagles as carrion birds. In Old Norse-Icelandic literature, the eagle is commonly associated with blood and death. Frank's conclusion is that "[d]eprived of its skaldic stanza, the rite of the blood-eagle has no viking-age support" (341).

In addition, Frank compares the grisly details of the blood eagle to descriptions of torture from late antiquity to the early Middle Ages, including the account of the torture of Saint Sebastian, who was led to a field and bound to a stake, so that archers could shoot arrows at him. According to his legend, so many arrows were shot that his ribs and internal organs were exposed. Frank proposes that these accounts of torture and martyrdom might well have inspired further exaggeration of Sighvat's half stanza into gruesome torture and a death ritual with no basis in reality. In her view, "[t]hirteenth-century Scandinavians were just doing what came naturally when they painted their ancestors bloodier-minded than they were" (343). Ronald Hutton (1991) supports Frank's suggestion that the blood eagle may owe at least some of its existence to Christian myth claiming that "[t]he hitherto notorious rite of the 'Blood Eagle', the killing of a defeated warrior by pulling up his ribs and lungs through his back, has been shown to be almost certainly a Christian myth resulting from the misunderstanding of some older verse" (282).

It should be noted, however, that elements of Frank's argument have been contested. Bjarni Einarsson (1998) draws attention to the Old Norse-Icelandic verb *skorit* (from infinitive *skera*), the last word in the half stanza in *Knútsdrápa*, arguing that this particular verb would not be used of the tearing of a corpse by an eagle and that instead the verb *slíta* would cover such an action. He also points out that "an eagle would not attack the back of a corpse" and that "eagles, vultures, ravens quite naturally prefer to go for the softer parts of the body or for gashes already made" (80–81). His conclusion is while Sighvat and his contemporaries "had ample opportunity to see how eagles, ravens and wolves behaved on battlefieds when the slaughter was over . . . they would not have been able to use the verb *skera* of the activity of any of them, while the notion of *skera bak* [cut the back] appears doubly impossible" (81). In his view, Sighvat and his contemporaries had never seen the blood-eagle slaughter, but "they had heard of it and believed in it as an ancient custom" (81).

Frank (1998) was not convinced by Bjarni Einarson's argument, however, and in response to his objections, she writes:

[E]ven on a naturalistic level Sighvatr's eagle behaves in an excruciatingly correct way. What was a poor bird to do when the only available corpse lay face down. My interpretation said nothing about eating. The bird is just standing there, digging in his heels and thinking. The rest varies with imagination. A back is turned in flight: surely a back cut down from behind provides a taste opportunity or two. Perhaps the eagle had poor eyesight and mistook Ella for a rabbit. (82)

PRIMARY DOCUMENT
BLOOD EAGLE AGAIN (1998)

Not all scholars have accepted Roberta Frank's argument. The Icelandic scholar Bjarni Einarsson was especially critical of Frank's reading of Knútsdrápa *and expressed reservations in an article, "De Normannorum atrociate, or On the Execution of Royalty by the Aquiline Method," which was published in* Saga-Book 22 (1988). *This caused Frank to respond in an article two years later, which gave rise to yet another lively debate between the two scholars in the same journal in 1998.*

IN A RECENT NOTE ('De Normannorum atrocitate, or on the execution of royalty by the aquiline method', *Saga-Book* 22, 1986, 79-82), Bjarni Einarsson takes polite exception 'as a native speaker of Icelandic' to my reading of two skaldic stanzas ('Viking atrocity and skaldic verse: the rite of the blood-eagle', *English historical review* 99, 1984, 332–43). His criticism of my handling of Kormakr's *lausavisa* 4 has already elicited a response (Klaus von See, 'At halsi Hagbaros,' *Skandinavistik 7,* 1987, 55-7). His objections to what I do to the first half-stanza of Sighvatr Pordarson's *Knutsdrapa* also deserve to be answered.

The verse in question is cryptic, knotty and allusive. When translated word for word into English the result is as follows:

Ok Ellu bak,	And Ella's back,
at, let hinn's sat,	at, had the one who dwelt,
Ivarr, ara,	Ivarr, with eagle,
Iorvik, skorit.	York, cut.

The syntax, in addition to being skewed, is ambiguous. Yet a chain of authors from the end of the twelfth century to the present agrees that these twelve words document a viking method of execution known as the blood-eagle sacrifice, a peculiar ceremony, that gets more inventive and sensational as time goes on. My article affirmed that Ella's back might just possibly have been incised with the picture of an eagle ('And Ivarr, who dwelt at York, had Ella's back cut with an eagle'), it was far more likely to have been lacerated by a real one ('Ivarr had Ella's back cut *by* an eagle'). Viking-age skalds were not reluctant to see men falling under the eagle's talons; the ellipsis in Sighvatr's verse—the skald's omission of claws—reflected, I argued, the demands of his terse metre, a speciality of Cnut's Anglo-Scandinavian court. Too optimistically, perhaps, I concluded that 'an experienced reader of skaldic poetry, looking at Sighvatr's stanza in isolation from its saga context, would have trouble seeing it as anything but a conventional utterance, an allusion to the eagle as carrion beast, the pale bird with red claws perched on and slashing the backs of the slain'.

But Bjarni, and his word carries weight, now tells us that 'no experienced Icelandic reader of skaldic poetry could possibly agree'. His chief reason for rejecting my interpretation is that in Icelandic, both early and late, the use of the verb *skera*, 'cut', to refer to carrion beasts ripping into bodies 'by claw, tooth and neb' is 'inconceivable'.

Bjarni will have to have a word with the author of *Stjorn* (ca 1310), who seems unaware of this prohibition. Indeed, this anonymous writer uses *skera* three times to describe the cutting action of claws. Panthers, he explains, give birth only once, because the cubs' claws tear their mother's womb, making it unfit for future conceptions: [they] '*skera* sva ok slita allan hennar kvid *medr sinum klom* ok allan getnadarliminn' ('thus they cut and slash all her womb and genitalia with their claws'; *Stjorn*, ed. C.R. Unger, 1862, 80/11, cited J. Fritzner, *Ordbog over det gamle norske Sprog*, 1883-96, III, p. 311; the words in italics translate Isidore's *unguibus lacerant, Etym.* XII, i, ii). The author of *Stjorn* does not hesitate to call the panther's damaged parts *skornir* (80/16) and he cites Pliny as authority for the fact that animals with sharp claws cannot have babies frequently because their insides are cut and damaged by their offspring *(skerast ok skemmast,* 80/19). Present-day Icelanders may not be able to say *hroefugl skar na,* but their brothers in Norway still can and do; and, as far as semantics is concerned, modem Norwegian is not necessarily more distant from Old Norse than modern Icelandic is.

It is, of course, an undeniable advantage to have Icelandic as mother tongue. Even native speakers, however, must recognize that the very process of 'education'—in its etymological sense—is one of separation from their matrix, of each generation making sense of things anew. If you ask speakers of contemporary American English what Juliet wanted to know when she murmured 'O Romeo, Romeo! wherefore art thou Romeo?' they will tell you she was inquiring into Romeo's whereabouts, rather than pondering 'Why are you Romeo and not Peter, or Michael, or Richard?' Bjarni, using his *Oxford English dictionary* as I wield my Fritzner, would, of course, never make this mistake, for he did not first hear this line in early childhood and—forced to make sense of an archaic or poetic locution—decide that Juliet is asking Romeo to reveal where he is hiding.

The distortion of language in skaldic verse brings out, in a similar way, the meaning-maker in man. It is precisely because *skera* usually means 'to cut' (with knife, sword, or ship's prow) that generations of Icelandic commentators, inspired by Sighvatr's allusiveness and metaphoric shorthand, detected a half-veiled hint of atrocity *in* his verse. But the eleventh-century skald no more intended to execute Ella by the 'aquiline method' than Shakespeare meant young Romeo to play hide-and-seek. I persist in the belief, which is not mine alone, that the conventions and workings of the earlier verse were not always perfectly understood, not even by the Icelandic saga-authors who quarried it for historical information. The conclusion of my article, limited and hedged around with doubts, still stands: 'Deprived of its skaldic stanza, the rite of the blood-eagle has no viking-age support.'

Source: Frank, Roberta. 1988. "The Blood-Eagle Again." *Saga-Book* 22: 287–289. Used by permission of the Viking Society for Northern Research.

Further Reading

de Vries, Jan. 1956. *Altgermanische Religionsgeschichte*, 2 vols. Berlin: Walter de Gruyter.

Einarsson, Bjarni. 1998. "*Blóðörn*—An Observation on the Ornithological Aspect." *Saga-Book* 23: 80–81.

Frank, Roberta. 1984. "Viking Atrocity and Skaldic Verse: The Rite of the Blood-Eagle." *The English Historical Review* 99: 332–343.

Frank, Roberta. 1998. "Ornithology and the Interpretation of Skaldic Verse." *Saga-Book* 23: 81–83.

Hutton, Ronald. 1991. *The Pagan Religions of the Ancient British Isles: Their Nature and Legacy*. Oxford: Blackwell.

Keary, C. F. 1891. *The Vikings in Western Christendom A.D. 789 to A.D. 888*. New York: Putnam's Sons.

Smyth, Alfred P. 1977. *Scandinavian Kings in the British Isles, 850–880*. Oxford: Oxford University Press.

Turville-Petre, E. O. G. 1964. *Myth and Religion of the North: The Religion of Ancient Scandinavia*. New York: Holt, Rinehart and Winston.

11

Vikings Drank Out of Skull Cups

What People Think Happened

The faulty idea that Vikings drank out of cups made from skulls has its origin in a line in stanza 25 of the skaldic poem *Krákumál* (the *Lay of Kraka*), which was purportedly recited by Ragnar Shaggy-Breeches as he lay dying after having been cast into a snake pit by the Northumbrian king Ella (d. 867). The line in question contains a kenning (poetic circumlocution), which Danish physician and antiquary Ole Worm (1588–1654) misinterpreted in his 1636 Latin translation. Worm translated the line as "we shall drink beer out of the sculls of our enemies" (Percy 1763, 40), instead of "soon shall we drink ale out of the curved branches of the skull" (Blackwell 1847, 105). Rather than referring to drinking vessels made of skulls, the "curved branches" allude to horns attached to a skull. In other words, Ragnar and his companions were drinking out of drinking horns, and not out of skulls.

The only other reference to skulls used as cups is in the eddic poem *Vǫlundarkviða* (the *Lay of Volund*). The poem relates that the smith Volund, who had been captured and hamstrung by King Nidud, was forced to craft magical items for the king. Eventually, Volund escaped, and as part of his revenge, he killed the king's two sons and made gem-encrusted cups out of their skulls to give to the king. A scene containing a similar act of revenge is found in *Vǫlsunga saga* (the *Saga of the Volsungs*), which tells that Gudrun killed her and Atli's sons and gave their hearts and blood to Atli to eat and drink. The instance of skull cups in *Vǫlundarkviða* is a literary invention to emphasize the brutality of Volund's revenge against King Nidud. However, it was Ole Worm's translation of the line in *Krákumál* that spawned the popular misconception of Vikings drinking out of skull cups.

How the Story Became Popular

Ole Worm's translation of *Krákumál* from Old Norse into Latin was in turn translated into other languages, along with the mistranslated line. Thomas Percy's 1763 translation into English contains the fateful misinterpretation ("we shall drink Beer out of the sculls of our enemies," 40). More translations followed, including Bertel Christian Sandvig's Danish translation (1779), Hugh Dowman's and James Johnstone's English translations (1781 and 1782), Friedrich David Graeter's German translation (1789), and William Herbert's English translation (1806). Interestingly, in Jean-Benjamin de La Borde's 1780 French rendition, the line in question is translated correctly, though it seems to have gone unnoticed or been ignored by many later translators. The idea of Vikings drinking from skull cups also found its way into other scholarly works. For example, A. S. Cottle's 1797 *Poetic Edda* translation, *Icelandic Poetry, Or The Edda of Saemund Translated into English Verse* contains a poem by Robert Southey that also references skull cups: "Of Ella, in the shield-roof's hall they thought / One day from Ella's skull to quaff the mead" (xxix).

Although I. A. Blackwell wrote in his revision of *Northern Antiquities, Or, An Historical Account of the Manners, Customs, Religion and Laws, Maritime Expeditions and Discoveries, Language and Literature of the Ancient Scandinavians* (1847) that the myth of the skull cups had been officially debunked by Danish runologist Finn Magnusen and Danish professor and antiquarian Carl Christian Rafn in 1826. Nonetheless, the misconception seems to have stuck, since Jón Stefánsson lamented the continued appearance of English translations with the misinterpreted kenning. He comments that "it seems still to be believed in England that the old heroes drank beer and mead out of the skulls of their enemies," and adds that "though it has been corrected time and again, the English seem never to learn the truth" (1891, 9). In a review in volume 206 of *The Gentleman's Magazine* (1859) of F. G. Bergmann's *Les Scythes, les Ancêtres des Peuples, Germaniques et Slaves* (1858), the reviewer claims that: "[t]he Scythian custom of drinking immoderately, and of drinking healths to their gods and to their deceased friends from cups made of the skulls of their enemies, ornamented with rims of gold, have been but too well followed by the Scandinavians" (188). Similarly, it is stated in an article in the July 5, 1877 issue of *Bow Bells* magazine that "[a]mong the Scandinavian barbarians it was deemed the highest point of felicity that they should, in the future state, be seated in the Hall of Odin, and there get intoxicated by quaffing strong liquors from the skulls of those over whom they had triumphed in battle" (31). The idea of Vikings drinking from the skulls of their enemies became an irresistible part of the romanticized image of the Vikings in the 19th century. It is possible that the correct translations of the line in *Krákumál* were deliberately ignored in order to make the image of the Vikings more compelling.

Skulls as drinking vessels found their way into works of fiction as well. In Matthew Arnold's poem *Balder Dead* (1855), which recounts the mythological episode of Baldr's death, it is told that in Valhalla, wine is served in both drinking horns and skulls: "And on the table stood the untasted meats, / And in the horns and gold-rimmed skulls the wine" (136). Charles Carrol Bombaugh remarked in 1867: "to this strange banqueting there are allusions without end to be met with in our literature" (479). In John R. Carling's novel *The Viking Skull* (1903), drinking cups made of skulls also play a central role. In the 20th century, the skull cup misconception began to decline, though references to and depictions of skull cups still appear. René Goscinny and Albert Uderzo's comic book *Astérix et les Normands* (1966), published in English as *Asterix and the Normans* (1978), depicts the Vikings with stereotypical horned helmets, fur clothing, and skull cups making an appearance in two scenes (9–10, 17). Finally, video games have also on occasion perpetuated the idea of Vikings drinking out of skull cups. In the "Viking Conquest" (Reforged Edition) expansion of the computer game "Mount & Blade: Warband" (2010), a skull cup appears in one scene. Mostly, however, drinking horns have come to replace skull cups.

PRIMARY DOCUMENT

THE DEATH-SONG OF RAGNAR LODBRACH (1781)

Among several English translations of Ole Worm's Latin translation of Krákumál *is Hugh Downman's 1781 translation,* The Death-Song of Ragnar Lodbrach, or Lodbrog, King of Denmark. *Stanza 25 contains the line with Worm's mistranslation, which has been retained in the English translation and perpetuates the misconception of Vikings drinking from the skulls of their enemies.*

I.
With our sword's resistless might
We have thinn'd the ranks of fight.

In early life, his volum'd train
The crested serpent roll'd in vain.
Thora's charms, the matchless prize;
Gothland saw my fame arise.
Thronging crouds the monster scan,
Shouts applausive hail me Man.
All his fierceness prompt to try,
The shaggy vestment cloth'd my thigh:
Soon transpierced, in death he lay,
My falchion smote for splendid pay.

II.
Still a youth, we steer our course,
T'ward the morning's distant source;
Through the vast Oreonic flood
Torrents run of crimson blood.
The yellow-footed bird we feast,
Plenty fills the ravenous beast.
Our steel-struck helms sublime resound,
The sea is all one bleeding wound.
Our foes lie weltering on the shore,
Deep the raven wades in gore.

III.
Crown'd with twenty rolling years,
High we raise our glittering spears,
And deeds of glorious worth display,
Wherever shines the lamp of day.
Still we the trembling east appall,
Eight mighty chiefs at Dimen fall.
We scorn with mean and niggard food,
To treat the generous eagle brood.
The wound its ruddy sweat distills,
The gaping ocean carnage fills.
Their host is struck with dire dismay,
Its strength of years dissolves away.

IV.
War and death terrific lower
When th' Helsingians brave our power:

We urge them down the gloomy road,
They throng t'ward Odin's dark abode.
The Vistula beheld our course,
Our navy stem its rapid force,
The biting sword descended steep,
One wound extensive glow'd the deep:
Its shores the reeking current died,
Our falchions mock'd their armor's pride
With echoing voices roar'd amain,
And cleft their stubborn shields in twain.

V.
No warrior droop'd, no warrior fled,
Till on the deck Heraudus bled.
A braver chief, to distant lands
Ne'er guided his victorious bands
Ne'er beheld a chief more brave
His ships of battle plough the wave.
His art impell'd by conscious might,
With eager transport fought the fight.

VI.
Their shields aside each warrior threw;
The spear on rapid pinion flew
Heroes its deadly speed contest,
It quiver'd in the dauntless breast.
With hunger keen the trenchant sword
Wide the Scarfian rocks engor'd.
His shield became of purple grain
E'er Rafno fell, the king of men.
From every helm-encircled crown,
The blood warm sweat in streams ran down.

VII.
Round th' Indirian isles that day
The crows were surfeited with prey.
There the wild beast inglutted stood,
For plenteous was the feast of blood.
All fought as one, no single name
Claim'd the distinguish'd mark of fame.

When first appear'd day's flaming star,
I saw the piercing darts of war.
The barbed arrows took their flight
When first he streak'd the east with light.

VIII.
Our swords loud-bellow'd o'ver the slain
Till Eislin fell on Laneo's plain.
Thence enrich'd with golden spoil,
War to our routed foemen's soil
We bring: where helmets throng'd the field
The falchion cut the pictured shield;
Their necks deep-pierc'd, with must abound,
It flows their cloven brains around.

IX.
Drench'd in blood our shields we rear,
The oil of blood anoints our spear.
In the Boringholmian bay
Making its quick tempestuous way,
The cloud of darts was onward borne,
Our targets were in sunder torn.
The bows their iron shower expel,
In the fierce conflict Volnir fell.
No king on earth could him exceed,
In valour and heroic deed.
Wide o'er the land the slaughter'd lay,
The howling beasts embrac'd their prey.

X.
The battle rag'd with heighten'd lust,
E'er princely Freyer bit the dust.
His breast plate's golden mail of yore
The hard blue sword, insteep'd in gore,
Conflicting with our warrior host,
Had hewn upon the Flandrian coast.
The virgin struck with woe appears
When she that morning's carnage hears,
A copious banquet we had given
To the fierce wolf, and birds of heaven.

XI.
Gasping in death these eyes survey'd,
An hundred times an hundred laid.
In haste we sail'd, a dreadful band,
To combat on Ænglane's land:
Six following days the rising sun
Beheld the strife of swords begun,
And six succeeding evenings close,
Till prostrate fall our vanquish'd foes,
Urg'd by our steel to sink in sight,
Valdiofur confess'd its might.

XII.
The rain of blood our falchions pour,
It smokes on Bardafyrdea's shore.
Doom'd to the hawks a pallid crowd,
The murmuring string was twang'd aloud.
Then where i Odin's deathful fight
The greedy sword, with eager bite,
Devour'd the cuirass, there the bow,
The casque, the morion, swiftly flow,
The bow with poison sharp to wound,
With sanguine sweat besprinkled round.

XIII.
The sport of war intent to try,
We rear our magic shields on high.
In Hiadningia's heroic play.
The vengeful swords whirl'd o'er the main
Their strong-knit bucklers tear in twain;
With mingled clash our arms resound,
The helms of men to dust are ground.
Not with more transport by his side
The lover clasps his beauteous bride.

XIV.
The thick-rais'd storm our shields defy;
In Northumbria's land they lie,
Their gory carcasses bestrew

The soil, and taint the morning dew,
Routed they fled with wild dismay,
Their boasted warriors dar'd nor stay,
Where the sword with grim delight
Their helmets polish'd plains would bite.
The genial bed such rapture warms,
Blest with the youthful widow's charms.

XV.
Herthiofe escap'd our force,
And widely sped his prosperous course,
Where with rude rocks against the skies
The southern Orcades arise,
While he who gave us, to display,
And shine in victory's bright array,
Rogvald, our glory and our pride,
Compell'd by fate's stern mandate, died.
Plung'd in the storm of arms he fell;
Then mourn'd the hawks with shrieking yell.
For dreadful in the sport of war,
The darts of blood he well could wield,
The shatter'd helms bestrew'd the field.

XVI.
Heaps pil'd on heaps the warriors lie,
The hawk looks down with joyous eye,
The pastime sees, and clotted gore,
Envying the eagle, nor the boar.
Together rush the shield and sword,
Then fell Irlandia's haughty lord,
Marstan; he floats in Vedra's bay,
The hungry raven's destined prey.

XVII.
Amid the weapons strifeful scorn,
Many a hero, in the morn
Of life and glory, press'd the plain.
My son, mature in fame, was slain.
Ripe in renown the dust he press'd,

The griding falchion rived his breast,
By Egill, dauntless Agner dies,
He rends his arms, the victor's prize.
In Hamdus' corselet sounds the lance,
Red lightnings from the standards glance.

XVIII.
Sparing of words, the brave I view;
Their foes they prodigally slew,
Thrown to the wolves; th' Endilian flood
For seven whole days was stain'd with blood.
So looks the wine our handmaids bear,
Died deep the impurpled ships appear.
The falchion raging mid th' alarms,
And hoarse tumultuous din of arms,
Gash'd many a mailed cuirass bright,
In Scioldungia's fatal fight.

XIX.
I saw the widow's darling joy,
I saw the virgin's fair-hair'd boy,
Saw them in morning beauty gay,
Saw set in death their youthful ray.
Warm with many a glowing stream,
Ila's ruddy billows gleam,
As by circling nymphs supplied,
The fervid bath, in copious tide,
From the vine's nectareous hoard,
Floats around the social board.
E'er Orn expir'd, with frequent stroke,
I saw his blood-stain'd buckler broke;
By strong necessity control'd,
Inverted life forsakes the bold.

XX.
The game of slaughtering swords, we haste,
Where Lind frowns o'er the watery waste,
With three contending kings to try;
How few escape rejoic'd to fly!

The wild beasts gnarring throng the strand,
The hawk and wolf commingled stand,
Tear them with goading hunger's fire,
Nortill with carnage cramm'd, retire.
While fierce we smote, th' Hybernian's blood,
With copious torrents swell'd the flood.

XXI.
The steel's sharp fang, and bite severe
The buckler prov'd; the whizzing spear,
Speeding to its direction true,
The breast-plate chased of golden hue.
On ugs will mark for many an age
The traces of that battle's rage.
There march'd the kings with eager feet
Intent the sport of swords to meet.
The crimson'd isle, on all its coast
Saw the red foaming billows tost.
Or from the desperate fight rebounds,
A flying dragon full of wounds.

XXII.
The brave with ardour yield their breath,
Nor heed the sure approach of death;
The thought of death their bosom warms,
They meet it in the storm of arms,
He oft deplores this fickle state,
Who never dar'd the frowns of fate.
Lur'd by the cheek of pallid fear
The joyful eagle hovers near,
The coward, to himself a pest,
Forbids the shield to guard his breast.

XXIII.
This I establish just and right,
That hurrying on to closest fight,
Youth against youth, with fervent heat,
Should rush, nor man from man retreat.
Long time was this the hero's pride;
And all who by the virgin's side

Aspire to lie, and taste her charms,
Should nobly stem the roar of arms.

XXIV.
Doubtless the fates our actions lead,
Beyond their limits none can tread.
Little of yore did I foresee,
That Ella would my death foresee,
When half-expiring with my wound,
Anxious I threw my garb around;
Conceal'd it from the warrior train,
And launch'd my vessels on the main:
Then over all the Scotian flood
We gave the beasts of prey their food.

XXV.
Hence springing in my thoughtful mind,
A never failing joy I find;
For well I know superbly graced,
For me the lofty seat is placed,
For me the gen'rous mead shall foam
In father Balder's festal dome:
From goblets pour'd its copious tide
By skulls of recreant foes supplied.
The brave shall ne'er lament their death
In Odin's splendid courts beneath;
No clamours vain I thither bear,
No sickly murmurs of despair.

XXVI.
Aslanga's sons would soon draw nigh,
With utmost swiftness hither fly,
And arm'd with falchions gleaming bright
Prepare the bitter deeds of fight,
If told, or could they but divine
What woe, what dire mischance is mine,
How many serpents round me hang,
And tear my flesh with poisonous fang;
A mother to my sons I gave,
With native worth who stamp'd them brave,

XXVII.

Fast to th' hereditary end,
To my allotted goal I tend.
Fix'd is the viper's mortal harm;
Within my heart, his mansion warm,
In the recesses of my breast
The writhing snake hath form'd his nest,
Yet Odin may in vengeance spread
The bloody scourge o'er Ella's head,
My son's fierce anger, at the tale,
Shall change to red, from deadly pale.
The fiery youths, at my decease,
Shall starting shun the seat of peace.

XXVIII.

Full fifty times I trod the field,
My standard rear'd, and poised my shield,
War's willing guest; nor deem'd the force
Of human hand would check my course.
Panting to gain a matchless name,
And soar o'er every king in fame,
For well in earliest years I taught
My sword to drink the crimson draught,
The sisters now my steps invite;
Unmoved I quit the realms of light.

XXIX.

Warn'd from within—break off the lay!
Th' inviting Sisters chide my stay.
By Odin sent, I hear their call,
They bid me to his fatal hall.
With them high-throned, the circling bowl
Of foaming mead shall chear my soul,
With joy I yield my vital breath,
And laugh in the last pangs of death.

Source: Wormius, Olaus. 1781. *The Death-Song of Ragnar Lodbrach, or Lodbrog, King of Denmark. Translated from the Latin of Olaus Wormius*, by Hugh Downman. London: Fielding and Walker. 7–36.

What Really Happened

Literary and archaeological evidence confirm that drinking was an important part of Norse culture during the Viking Age, but aside from the scene in *Vǫlundarkviða*, which is probably no more than a literary invention, there is no evidence of the use of skull cups in Scandinavia. Most people during the Viking Age used wooden cups or cattle horns for drinking; the latter often had a metal tip and strip of decorated metal around the brim. Cups and bowls made of metal were also used, and some of the more affluent people even drank out of expensive imported glass cups and beakers (Foote and Wilson 1970, 167). A scene in *Haralds saga hárfagra* (the *Saga of Harald Fairhair*) describes the drinking vessels on the table of the wealthy farmer Áki when he receives and holds a feast in honor of King Harald Fairhair of Norway (850–933) and King Eirik Eymundsson of Sweden (d. 882):

> Now when the kings came to the feast, King Eirik with his court was taken into the old hall; but Harald with his followers into the new hall. The same difference was in all the table furniture, and King Eirik and his men had the old-fashioned vessels and horns, but all gilded and splendid; while Harald and his men had entirely new vessels and horns adorned with gold, all with carved figures, and shining like glass: and both companies had the best of liquor. (358–59)

Archaeological finds have confirmed the existence of decorated drinking horns and metal and glass vessels. A small silver cup with ornately engraved animal decorations found in Jelling—after which a style of art is named—may have been used in feasts or possibly for Communion during Christian ceremonies (Wilson 1966, 95). Additionally, there are visual representations of drinking vessels from the Viking Age that are also clearly not skulls. For example, the Viking Age picture stones from Hunninge and Tjängvide on Gotland both depict a female figure welcoming a mounted horse rider with a drinking horn in the top panel. On the Swedish mainland, the runestone U 1163 also depicts a female figure bearing a drinking horn, probably representing a scene in *Vǫlsunga saga* in which the Valkyrie Sigrdrifa welcomes Sigurd. One final example is the small silver figures of women bearing drinking horns or cups, such as the ones found at Birka in Sweden and on Öland. There are many clues as to the types of drinking vessels used in the material and visual culture of Viking Age Scandinavia, but none indicates or suggests that the Vikings used the skulls of their enemies as cups.

Although there is no evidence from Scandinavia, it is true that skulls have been used as cups in various parts of the world at different times. In 2011, a team of archaeologists in London analyzed three skulls approximately 14,700 years old, discovered in Gough Cave in Somerset, England, and concluded that they had been deliberately fashioned into drinking vessels, perhaps to be used in ceremonies (2011, 994). In light of this discovery, maybe the particularly English obsession with Vikings drinking out of skull cups might have deeper roots.

PRIMARY DOCUMENT
SAGA OF EGIL SKALLA-GRIMSSON (CA. 1240)

This excerpt from Egils saga Skalla-Grímssonar (*the* Saga of Egil Skalla-Grimsson) *relates that Egil enjoys the hospitality of a man named Bard. However, Egil drinks so much that he incites the wrath of his hosts, who attempt to put an end to the situation by giving him a drinking horn filled with poisoned ale. Egil suspects foul play and carves magic runes on the horn, which immediately bursts apart. Egil recites an angry verse, chaos ensues, and the feast ends in spilled ale, blood, and vomit.*

King Eric and queen Gunnhilda came that same evening to Atla-isle, and Bard had prepared there a banquet for the king; and there was to be there a sacrifice to the guardian spirits. Sumptuous was the banquet, and great the drinking within the hall.

'Where is Bard?' asked the king; 'I see him not.'

Someone said: 'Bard is outside supplying his guests.'

'Who be these guests,' said the king, 'that he deemeth this more a duty than to be here within waiting on us?'

The man said that some house-carles of lord Thorir were come thither.

The king said: 'Go after them at once, and call them in hither.'

And so it was done, with the message that the king would fain see them.

Whereupon they came. The king received Aulvir well, and bade him sit in the high-seat facing himself, and his comrades outside him. They did so, Egil sitting next to Aulvir. Ale was then served to them to drink. Many toasts went round, and a horn should be drunk to each toast.

But as the evening wore on, many of Aulvir's companions became helpless. Some remained in the room, though sick, some went out of doors.

Bard busily plied them with drink. Then Egil took the horn which Bard had offered to Aulvir, and drank it off. Bard said that Egil was very thirsty, and brought him at once the horn again filled, and bade him drink it off. Egil took the horn, and recited a stave:

'Wizard-worshipper of cairns!
Want of ale thou couldst allege,
Here at spirits' holy feast.
False deceiver thee I find.
Stranger guests thou didst beguile,
Cloaking thus thy churlish greed.
Bard, a niggard base art thou,
Treacherous trick on such to play.'

Bard bade him drink and stop that jeering. Egil drained every cup that came to him, drinking for Aulvir likewise. Then Bard went to the queen and told her there was a man there who put shame on them, for, howsoever much he drank, he still said he was thirsty. The queen and Bard then mixed the drink with poison, and bare it in. Bard consecrated the cup, then gave it to the ale-maid. She carried it to Egil, and bade him drink. Egil then drew his knife and pricked the palm of his hand. He took the horn, scratched runes thereon, and smeared blood in them. He sang:

'Write we runes around the horn,
Redden all the spell with blood;
Wise words choose I for the cup
Wrought from branching horn of beast.
Drink we then, as drink we will,
Draught that cheerful bearer brings,
Learn that health abides in ale,
Holy ale that Bard hath bless'd.'

The horn burst asunder in the midst, and the drink was spilt on the straw below. Then Aulvir began to be faint. So Egil stood up, took Aulvir by the hand, and led him to the door. Egil shifted his cloak to his left side, and under the mantle held his sword. But when they came to the door, then came Bard after them with a full horn, and bade them drink a farewell cup. Egil stood in the door. He took the horn and drank it off; then recited a stave:

'Ale is borne to me, for ale
Aulvir now maketh pale.
From ox-horn I let pour
'Twixt my lips the shower.
But blind they fate to see
Blows thou bring'st on thee:
Full soon from Odin's thane
Feel'st thou deadly rain.'

With that Egil threw down the horn, but gripped his sword and drew; it was dark in the room. He thrust Bard right through the middle with the sword, so that the point went out at the back. Bard fell dead, the blood welling from the wound. Aulvir fell too, vomiting. Then Egil dashed out of the room; it was pitch dark outside. Egil at once ran off from the buildings. But in the entrance-room it was now seen that Bard and Aulvir were fallen.

Then came the king, and bade them bring light; whereupon they saw what had happened, that Aulvir lay there senseless; but Bard was slain, and the floor all streaming with blood. Then the king asked where was that big man who had drunk most that evening. Men said that he had gone out.

Source: Green, W. C., trans. 1893. *The Story of Egil Skallagrimsson: Being an Icelandic Family History of the Ninth and Tenth Centuries.* London: E. Stock. 75–77.

THE BEGUILING OF GYLFI (CA. 1220)

In this excerpt from Snorri Sturluson's Gylfaginning (*the* Beguiling of Gylfi), *Thor and Loki travel to the land of the giants, where Thor is made to compete against giants in various tasks. One such task is a drinking competition with an enormous drinking horn. After completing all his trials seemingly unsatisfactorily, Útgarda-Loki reveals he has tricked Thor, who has proven himself stronger than the giants had imagined. As in* Egils saga Skalla-Grímssonar, *the drinking vessel used is a horn.*

XLVI. "Thor turned forward on his way, and his fellows, and went onward till mid-day. Then they saw a castle standing in a certain plain, and set their necks down on their backs before they could see up over it. They went to the cattle; and there was a grating in front of the castle-gate, and it was closed. Thor went up to the grating, and did not succeed in opening it; but when they struggled to make their way in, they crept between the bars and came in that way. They saw a great hall and went thither; the door was open; then they went in, and saw there many men on two benches, and most of them were big enough. Thereupon they came before the king Útgarða-Loki and saluted him; but he looked at them in his own good time, and smiled scornfully over his teeth, and said: 'It is late to ask tidings of a long journey; or is it otherwise than I think: that this toddler is Öku-Thor? Yet thou mayest be greater than thou appearest to me. What manner of accomplishments are those, which thou and thy fellows think to be ready for? No one shall be here with us who knows not some kind of craft or cunning surpassing most men.'

. . . .

"Next, Útgarða-Loki asked Thor what feats there were which he might desire to show before them: such great tales as men have made of his mighty works. Then Thor answered that he would most willingly undertake to contend with any in drinking. Útgarða-Loki said that might well be; he went into the hall and called his serving-boy, and bade him bring the sconce-horn which the henchmen were wont to drink off. Straightway the serving-lad came forward with the horn and put it into Thor's hand. Then said Útgarða-Loki: 'It is held that this horn is well drained if it is drunk off in one drink, but some drink it off in two; but no one is so poor a man at drinking that it fails to drain off in three.' Thor looked upon the horn, and it did not seem big to him; and yet it was somewhat long. Still he was very thirsty; he took and drank, and swallowed enormously, and thought that he should not need to bend oftener to the horn. But when his breath failed, and he raised his head from the horn and looked to see how it had gone with the drinking, it seemed to him that there was very little space by which the drink was lower now in the horn than before. Then said Útgarða-Loki: 'It is well drunk, and not too much; I should not have believed, if it had been told me, that Ása-Thor could not drink a greater draught. But I know that thou wilt wish to drink it off in another draught.' Thor answered nothing; he set the horn to his mouth, thinking now that he should drink a greater drink, and struggled with the draught until his breath gave out; and yet he saw that the tip of the horn would not come up so much as he liked. When he took the horn from his mouth and looked into it, it seemed to him then as if it had decreased less than the former time; but now there was a clearly apparent lowering in the horn. Then said Útgarða-Loki: 'How now, Thor? Thou wilt not shrink from one more drink than may he well for thee? If thou now drink the third draught from the horn, it seems to me as if this must he esteemed the greatest; but thou canst not be called so great a man here among us as the Æsir call thee, if thou give not a better account of thyself in the other games than it seems to me may come of this.' Then Thor became angry, set- the horn to his mouth, and drank with all his might, and struggled with the drink as much as he could; and when he looked into the horn, at least some space had been made. Then he gave up the horn and would drink no more.

"Then said Útgarda-Loki: Now it is evident that thy prowess is not so great as we thought it to be;"

. . .

". . . when thou didst drink from the horn, and it seemed to thee to go slowly, then, by my faith, that was a wonder which I should not have believed possible: the other end of the horn was out in the sea, but thou didst not perceive it. But now, when thou comest to the sea, thou shalt be able to mark what a diminishing thou hast drunk in the sea: this is henceforth called "ebb-tides.""

". . . And now it is truth to tell that we must part; and it will be better on both sides that ye never come again to seek me. Another time I will defend my castle with similar wiles or with others, so that ye shall get no power over me.'"

Source: Sturluson, Snorri. 1916. *The Prose Edda*, translated by Arthur Gilchrist Brodeur. New York: The American-Scandinavian Foundation. 61–68.

Further Reading

Arnold, Matthew. 1877. "Balder Dead." In *Poems*. London: Macmillan and Co. 136–189.

Bombaugh, Charles Carroll. 1867. *Gleanings from the Harvest Fields of Literature: A Melange of Excerpta, Curious, Humorous, and Instructive*. Baltimore: T. Newton Kurtz. 478–479.

Fjalldal, Magnús. 2015. "The Last Viking Battle." *Scandinavian Studies* 87(3): 317–331.

Foote, Peter, and David M. Wilson. 1970. *The Viking Achievement: The Society and Culture of Early Medieval Scandinavia*. London: Sidgwick & Jackson.

Johnstone, James, trans. 1782. *Lodbrokar-Quida; or the Death-Song of Lodbroc; now first correctly printed from various manuscripts, with a free English translation. To which are added, the various readings; a literal Latin version; an Islando-Latino glossary; and explanatory notes.* [Copenhagen]: Printed for the author.

Mallet, Paul Henri. 1847. *Northern Antiquities, or, An Historical Account of the Manners, Customs, Religion and Laws, Maritime Expeditions and Discoveries, Language and Literature of the Ancient Scandinavians*, translated by I. A. Blackwell. London: H.G. Bohn. 105.

Nylén, Erik. 1978. *Stones, Ships and Symbols: The Picture Stones of Gotland from the Viking Age and Before*. Stockholm: Gidlund.

Percy, Thomas, trans. 1763. "The Dying Ode of Regner Lodbrog." In *Five Pieces of Runic Poetry Translated from the Islandic Language: Quotations*. London: Printed for R. and J. Dodsley, in Pall-Mall. 27–42.

Rafn, Carl Christian. 1826. *Krakas Maal, eller Kvad om Kong Ragnar Lodbroks Krigsbedrifter og heltedød, efter en gammel skindbog og flere hidtil ubenyttede haandskrifter, med dansk, latinsk og fransk oversaettelse, forskjellige laesemaader, samt kritiske or philologiske anmaerkninger*. Copenhagen: Jens Hostrup Schultz.

Science. 2011. "Cheers! Ancient Britons Made Skull Cups." 331(6020): 994.

Stefánsson, Jón. 1891. "The Influence of the Norse upon English Literature in the Eighteenth and Nineteenth Centuries." *The Literary Digest*, 4(5): 9.

Sturluson, Snorri. 1889. Harald Harfager's Saga. In *The Heimskringla; Or, The Sagas of the Norse Kings from the Icelandic of Snorre Sturlason*, translated by Samuel Laing, Esq. Volume 1. London: J. C. Nimmo. 342–398.

Wilson, David M., and Ole Klindt-Jensen. 1966. *Viking Art*. London: George Allen and Unwin Ltd.

Bibliography

Arnold, Martin. 2006. *The Vikings: Culture and Conquest*. New York: Hambledon Continuum.

Barnes, Michael P. 2012. *Runes: A Handbook*. Woodbridge: Boydell.

Brink, Stefan, in collaboration with Neil Price, ed. 2012. *The Viking World*. London: Routledge.

Brøndsted, Johannes. 1965. *The Vikings*, translated by Kalle Skov. London: Penguin.

Chartrand, R., K. Durham, M. Harrison, and I. Hearth. 2006. *The Vikings: Voyagers of Discovery and Plunder*. Foreword by Magnus Magnusson. Oxford: Osprey Publishing.

Christiansen, Eric. 2002. *The Norsemen in the Viking Age*. Oxford: Blackwell.

DuBois, Thomas. 1999. *Nordic Religions in the Viking Age*. Philadelphia: University of Pennsylvania Press.

Fitzhugh, William W., and Elizabeth I. Ward, ed. 2000. *Vikings: The North Atlantic Saga*. Washington: Smithsonian Institution Press.

Fjalldal, Magnús. 2015. "The Last Viking Battle." *Scandinavian Studies* 87(3): 317–331.

Foote, Peter, and David M. Wilson. 1970. *The Viking Achievement: The Society and Culture of Early Medieval Scandinavia*. London: Sidgwick & Jackson.

Graham-Campbell, James. 1980. *The Viking World*. New Haven: Ticknor and Fields.

Graham-Campbell, James, and Dafydd Kidd. 1980. *The Vikings*. London: British Museum Publications.

Harty, Kevin J., ed. 2011. *The Vikings on Film: Essays on Depictions of the Nordic Middle Ages*. Jefferson, NC: McFarland.

Holman, Katherine. 2003. *Historical Dictionary of the Vikings*. Lanham, MD: Scarecrow Press.

Jesch, Judith. 1991. *Women in the Viking Age*. Woodbridge: Boydell Press.

Lines, Craig. 2014. "Why Is Cinema So Obsessed with Vikings?" Den of Geek. March 3. Accessed October 1, 2017. http://www.denofgeek.com/movies/vikings/29442/why-is-cinema-so-obsessed-with-vikings.

Magnusson, Magnus. 1980. *Vikings!* New York: E. P. Dutton.

Oliver, Neil. 2014. *The Vikings: A New History*. New York: Pegasus.

Orchard, Andy. 1997. *Dictionary of Old Norse Myth and Legend*. London: Cassell.

Page, R. I. 1995. *Chronicles of the Vikings: Records, Memorials, and Myths*. Toronto: University of Toronto Press.

Pulsiano, Phillip, and Kirsten Wolf, ed. 1993. *Medieval Scandinavia: An Encyclopedia*. New York: Garland Publishing.

Roesdahl, Else. 1991. *The Vikings*, translated by Susan M. Margeson and Kirsten Williams. London: Penguin.

Sawyer, P. H. 1971. *The Age of the Vikings*. 2nd edition. London: Edward Arnold Ltd.

Sawyer, P. H., ed. 1997. *The Oxford Illustrated History of the Vikings*. Oxford: Oxford University Press.

Simek, Rudolf. 1993. *Dictionary of Northern Mythology*, translated by Angela Hall. Cambridge: D. S. Brewer.

Swanton, Michael, trans. 2000. *The Anglo-Saxon Chronicles*. London: Phoenix Press.

Wawn, Andrew. 2000. *The Vikings and the Victorians: Inventing the Old North in Nineteenth-Century Britain*. Rochester, NY: D. S. Brewer.

Wilson, David M., and Ole Klindt-Jensen. 1966. *Viking Art*. London: George Allen and Unwin Ltd.

Winroth, Anders. 2014. *The Age of the Vikings*. Princeton: Princeton University Press.

Wolf, Kirsten. 2004. *Daily Life of the Vikings*. Westport, CT: Greenwood Press.

Index

Aachen, 69
Abbo of Fleury, 109, 111, 147
Adam of Bremen, x, 53–54, 56, 101
Aelfric of Eynsham, 109–111
Aethelred, King, 69
Aggersborg, 44
Al-Biruni, 118
Alcuin, 69
Allen, George Cantrell, 136
Al-Madjus, 26
Angers, 70
Anglo-Saxon Chronicle, x, 1, 16, 53, 70, 109, 148
Angouleme, 70
Annals of St-Bertin, x, 70
Ansgar, 59–60
Århus, 16, 43
Ari Thorgilsson, 31, 60
Arnold, Matthew, 157
Arrows, 71, 116
Aryan race, xi–xii, 3
Ascomanni, 26
Asterix and the Normans, 111, 157
Athelstan, King, 60–61
Athens, 79

Aud the Deep-Minded. *See* Unn the Deep-Minded
Axes, xiii, 71, 109–111, 116–117, 120

Baghdad, 124
Balder Dead, 157
Baldr, 55, 157
Ballentyne, R.M., 135
Baring-Gould, Sabine, 135
Barron, Elwyn A., 3
Barth, Justus, 3
Bayeux, 70
Bayeux tapestry, 117
Beauvais, 70
Beck, Ernest, 134
Belarus, 78
Beorhtric, 1
Bergmann, F.G., 156
Berserker, 4, 40, 127
Birka, 16–17, 43, 167
Birkeli, Fridtjov, 59
Bjarni Einarsson, 150–151
Björkö, 30, 59
Blackley, William Lewery, 55
Black Sea, ix, 15, 42

Blackwell, I.A, 55, 156
Blind, Karl, 138
Blood Eagle, 147
Blood eagle, carving of, viii, xi, 37, 145–147, 149–150
Bolli Bollason, 79
Bombaugh, Charles Carrol, 157
Bordeaux, 70
Borgnine, Ernest, 4
Bows, 116
Bresler, Jerry, 39
British Isles, vii, ix, xi, 15–16, 60, 69, 117
British Museum, xiii, 71–72
Brøgger, Anton Wilhelm, 95
Brøndsted, Johannes, 125
Browne, Dik, 111, 134
Brynjólfur Sveinsson, 54
Buckland, Paul C., 123–124
Byzantium, 15, 78–80

Carling, John R., 157
Caspian Sea, ix, 15, 43
The Champion of Odin: Or Viking Life in Days of Old, 2, 55
Charlemagne, 69, 77
Charles III the Simple, 77–78
Chartres, 70, 77
Children of Odin, 55
Christians, viii–ix, 53–56, 59–61, 69–70, 100, 167
Clinton, Hillary Rodham, 91
Clothing, 17, 157
Clubs, 109–111
Cnut, King, 146
Cockburn, Patrick, 71
Codex Regius, 44, 54, 16
Cogadh Gaedhel re Gallaibh, x, 70
Coins, 17
Computer games, vii, 4, 56, 157
Conical helmets, 136, 142
Constantinople, 17, 79
Conversion, 59–60

Copenhagen, 71
Cosmology, 54
Cottle, A.S., 156
Creed, Olivier, 27
Curtis, Tony, 4

Danegeld, 16
Danelaw, 16
Danevirke, vii, 44
De Gobineau, Joseph Arthur, 3
De moribus et actis primorum normanniae ducum, 77
Denmark, 15–16, 26, 31, 43–44, 53–54, 59, 61, 78–79, 94, 101, 157
De Vries, Jan, 146
Diemer, M. Zeno, 135
Disease, 126
Divorce, 100
Doepler, Carl Emil, 135
Dorestad, 70, 78
Douglas, Kirk, 4, 125
Dowman, Hugh, 156
Dróttkvætt, 45
Dublin, 16, 71, 94, 123
Dudo of Saint-Quentin, 77
Dumville, David, 71

Eadburh, 1
Eddic poetry, xi, 44, 54, 116, 125–126, 146, 149, 155–156, 167
Edmund, St, 109–111, 147
Egedius, Halfdan, 142
Egils saga Skalla-Grímsonar, 45, 61, 119, 168, 170
Eirik Eymundsson, King, 167
Eiríks saga rauða, 126
Eketorp, 43
Ella, King, 38, 145–146, 148, 151, 155–156
England, ix, 16, 26, 69, 77–78, 123, 125, 135, 138, 148–149, 156, 168
Erik Bloodaxe, King, 120

Erling the Bold, 135
Ermentarius, 69
Estonia, 15
Evreux, 70
Eyrbyggja saga, 125–127

Faroe Islands, ix, 15, 32, 95
Feathered helmets, 135
Female Viking warriors, 30–31
Fimmel, Travis, 4
Finland, 15, 27, 117
Five Pieces of Runic Poetry, 38
Foote, Peter, 70, 94
Fortifications, 43
Fortresses, vii, xii, 42–43
France, vii, ix, 15, 69, 77, 117
Frank, Roberta, 133, 135, 138, 146, 149–151
Frey, 53–55
Freyja, 53
Frisia, 70
Frithiofs saga, x–xi, 5, 55, 134, 136
Fyrkat, 44

Gaill, 26
Galt, Christopher, 147
Geatish Society. *See* Götiska förbundet
Geats, 2
Geijer, Erik Gustaf, x, 26–27
Germany, vii, ix, 3, 15, 69, 72, 111, 117, 125, 135, 147
Gesta Danorum, x, 135, 146–147
Gesta Hammaburgensis ecclesiae pontificum, x, 53, 56, 101
Goði, 101
Goethe, Johann Wolfgang von, xi
Gokstad ship, 43
Göngu-Hrólfs saga, 31, 77
Gothicism, 2
Goths, 2, 37
Götiska förbundet, x, 2, 5, 26
Gotland, 15, 17, 43–44, 147, 167

Graeter, Friedrich David, 156
Grágás, 1
Graves of the Northmen, 3
Gray, Thomas, 38
Greece, 78–79
Greenland, 123, 126
Grettir the Outlaw, 135
Grettis saga, 80
Grimm, Jacob, xi
Grimm, Wilhelm, xi
Gylfaginning. *See Prose Edda*

Hagan, Bob, 134
"Hagar the Horrible," 111, 134
Hagia Sophia, 17, 79
Hakon of Lade, Earl, 101
Hakon the Good, King, 60
Halfdan Longleg, 145
The Hall of Odin, 55
Harald Bluetooth, King, xi, 44, 53, 59
Harald Fairhair, King, 94, 145, 167
Harald Hard-Ruler Sigurdsson, King, 79–80
Haralds saga harðráða, 80
Haralds saga hárfagra, 167
Hávamál, 116, 125–126
Hebrides, 32, 77, 94, 126
Hedeby, 16, 43–44, 59
Heimskringla, 2, 79–80, 95, 136, 142, 145
Helmets. *See* Conical helmets; Feathered helmets; Horned helmets; Winged helmets
Herat, 118
Herbert, William, 156
Hird, 78
Hirst, Michael, 4, 147
Hitler, Adolf, xii
Holcomb, Thomas A.E. and Martha A Lyon, 55
Holland, Sir Henry, xi
Hordaland, 1

Horn, Frederik Winkel, 135
Horned helmets, viii, xi, 2, 26, 39–40, 72, 110–111, 124, 133–136, 157
Hrafnkels saga, 80
Hughes, Thomas, 55
Huginn, 135
Human sacrifice, 93, 124, 145–146, 149–150
Hutton, Ronald, 150
Hygiene, x, 37, 123–126

Ibn Fadlān, x, 124
Ibrāhīm ibn Y'a'qūb al-Turtushi, 125
Iceland, ix–xi, 15, 32, 60, 69, 94–95, 100–102, 124–127, 133
Idun, x
Iduna, x, 26, 136
Ingvar the Far-Traveled, 16
Inheritance, 93–95, 101
Ireland, 32, 94
Íslendingabók, 31, 60
Ivar the Boneless, 111, 145–146, 149

Jaroslav, Prince, 80
Javelins, 116
Jelling, 167
Jesch, Judith, 30
Jochens, Jenny, 101
Johnson, Runer, 111, 134
Johnstone, James, 156
Jón Stefánsson, 156

Kaupang, 16
Keary, C.V., 72, 146
Kenning, 38, 45, 155–156
Kiev, 16
Knives, 116
Knútsdrápa, 146, 149–151
Krákumál, 38, 40, 155–157
Krohg, Christian, 142

La Borde, Jean-Benjamin de, 156
Lamellar armor, 17
Landnámabók, 60
Language, 1–2, 15–16, 25–26, 30, 150
Latvia, 15
Laws, 1, 94, 101
Laxdæla saga, 61, 79, 92, 94–95, 102, 110, 116
Liberman, Anatoly, 25–26
Liljencrantz, Ottilie A., 110
Limoges, 70
Lindisfarne, ix, 16, 69
Lochlannach, 26
Logos nuthetikos, 79
Longfellow, Henry Wadsworth, 10
Longhouses, 123
Longships, vii, 4, 123
The Long Ships, 111
Lothar, Emperor, 78
Louis the German, 78

Magnusen, Finn, 156
Magnusson, Magnus, 91
Mallet, Paul Henry, 40, 54
Malmström, Gustav, 134, 136
Maritime technology, 42
Marschall, Edison, 124
McDonagh, Melanie, 71
Meaux, 70
Melun, 70
Metlesen, Wilhelm, 142
Miller, John B., 55
Minnesota Vikings, 133–134
Moe, Louis, 135
Montagy, Earl George, 37–38
Movies, vii, 3–4, 39–40, 55, 110–111, 124
Muckleston, Rowland, 55
Muninn, 135
Munthe, Gerhard, 142
Muslims, x

Mythical-heroic sagas, 31, 77, 118, 155, 167
Mythology, xi–xii, 3, 54, 138, 150

Nazis, xii, 3
Neoclassicism, 37
The Netherlands, vii, ix, 78
Nidaros, 60
Nietzsche, Friedrich, xi
Njáls saga, 80, 116
Noirmoutier, 69
Nonnebakken, 44
Nordmanni, 1, 26
Normandy, 31, 78
The Northmen: The Sea-Kings and Vikings, 2
Norway, 1, 4, 15, 31, 43, 59–60, 79, 93–94, 101, 117, 125, 142
Novels, 2–3, 55–56, 110, 124, 155
Nover, Jakob, 135
Novgorod, 16

Odin, xi–xii, 38, 44, 53–55, 116, 125–126, 135, 145, 147, 156
Odin, A Poem, 55
Odin's Sagas, 55
Offa, King, 1
Olaf Haraldsson, King, 59, 142
Olaf Tryggvason, King, 59, 61, 142
Öland, 43–44, 134, 167
Old East Norse, 15
Old Gutnish, 15
Old West Norse, 15
Orkneyinga saga, 17, 32, 145, 147
Orkney Islands, ix, 16–17, 32, 55, 95, 145
Orléans, 70
"Orms þáttr Stórólfssonar," 146
Oseberg burial mound, 93, 95
Oseberg ship, 43–44
Otto II, Emperor, 53

Parasites, 123–124
Paris, 70, 133
Passion of Saint Edmund, 109–111, 147
Passio Sancti Eadmundi, 109, 147
Percy, Thomas, 38–40, 55, 156
Périgueux, 70
Persia, 16, 118
Petersen, Eilif, 142
Philip Augustus, King, 78
Picture stones, 17, 44
Pinkerton, John, 2
Piraeus, 79
Place names, 16
Poetic Edda. *See* Eddic poetry
Poetry, x–xi, 5, 10, 26–27, 38–39, 42, 44–45, 54–55, 116, 125–126, 146, 155–157
Poland, 71
Polygamy, 101
Primo signatio, 61
Prose Edda, 54, 170

Rafn, Carl Christian, 156
Ragnar Lothbrok (Shaggy-Breeches), xi, 38, 40, 56, 111, 145, 148, 155, 157
Ragnarssona þáttr, 145, 147
Ramparts, vii, xii
Reginsmál, 146, 149
The Rhinegold, 3
Ribe, 16, 59
Ring of the Nibelungs, xi, 3, 135
Robinson, Thomas Heath, 136
Roesdahl, Else, 31, 123
Rollo, 31–32, 56, 77–78
Romantic nationalism, 2, 26, 39
Roric, 78
Rørik. *See* Roric
Rouen, 70
Rousseau, Jean-Jacques, 39
Runes, 55

Runestones, 16, 44–45, 59–60, 78, 93, 147, 167
Runic graffiti, 17
Runic inscriptions, 15, 59–60, 70, 78–79, 93–94
Rus, ix–x, xii, 26, 78, 102, 124
Russel, Craig, 147
Russia, ix–x, xii, 15–17, 27, 117, 124

Sacrifices, 54
Sagas of Icelanders, x, 32, 61, 71, 79–80, 92, 94, 100, 102, 110, 116, 119, 125–126
Sandvig, Bertel Christian, 156
Saunas, 125, 127
Sawyer, Birgit, 91, 93, 100
Sawyer, Peter, 71
Saxes, 116
Saxo Grammaticus, x, 135, 146
Scandinavia. *See* Denmark; Norway; Sweden
Scotland, 94
Sebastian, St., 150
Seine, 70
Shaw, Clement Burbank, 55
Shetland Islands, ix, 16
Shields, xiii
Sighvat Thordarson, 146, 149–150
Sigtuna, 59
Sigurd the Dragon-Slayer, 118, 146, 167
Skaldic poetry, 38, 44–45, 120, 146, 149
Skalla-Grímsson, Egill, 45, 168
The Skeleton in Armor, 10
Skuldelev ship, 43
Skull cups, viii, xi, 37–38, 124, 155–158
Slaves, 32, 71, 102, 124
Sleipnir, 44
Smyth, Alfred P., 147
Snorri Sturluson, 2, 54, 79–80, 95, 136, 142, 145, 170

Sonatorrek, 45
Song of Frithiof, 136
Southey, Robert, 156, 156
Souvenirs, 26–27, 133
Spain, 15, 125
Spears, xiii, 116
SS, 3, 71
Stalsberg, Anne, 117
Stamford Bridge, Battle of, ix
Standen, Clive, 56
Staraja Ladoga, 16
Stave churches, 4, 44
Stevens, George, 55
Stone carving, 16
Sturlunga saga, 100, 116
Supremacists, xii, 3
Sutherland, Alyssa, 56
Sweden, x, 2, 15, 17, 30–31, 54, 56, 59–60, 78, 93–94, 117, 134, 147, 167
Swords, xiii, 71, 110–111, 116–118

Tegnér, Esaias, x, xi, 5, 26, 55, 134, 136
Temples, 54
Thanet, 16
The 13th Warrior, 4
The Thrall of Leif the Lucky, 110
Thor, 53–54, 60–61, 170
Thorgeir Thorkelsson, 60
Torf-Einar, 145
Torsburg, 43
Tortosa, 125
Toulouse, 70
Tours, 70
Trade routes, xii, 15–16
Trading centers, xii, 16, 70, 78
Trelleborg, 44
Turville-Petre, E.O.G., 146
TV series, 4, 56, 111

Übermensch, xi
Ukraine, 78

INDEX

United States, xii, 133
Unn the Deep-Minded, 94–95
Uppsala, 54–56, 60
Urnes stave church, 44

Valhalla, 4, 55, 147, 157
Valhalla Rising, 4, 39
Valkyries, 40, 55, 135, 167
Varangian guard, 17, 78–80
Västergarn, 43
Vermondois, 77
Vicky the Viking, 111, 134
Victoria, Queen, xi
Victorians, xi, 3
Video games, 4, 40, 56, 157
"Viking" (etymology), 25
The Viking: film, 4, 26–27, 39, 55, 110; novel, 2–3, 124; poem, 26–27
Viking apologists, xii–xiii
The Viking Bride, 3
Vikingen, x, 26–27
The Viking Queen, 4
Viking raids, viii–ix, xiii, 1, 15–16, 30–32, 42, 53, 69, 71, 77, 110
Viking revisionists, xii–xiii, 71
Vikings, 4, 56, 147
The Vikings, 4, 39, 71, 124
The Viking's Daughter, 3

Viking ships, 32
The Viking Skull, 157
Viking Society, 95
Viktor the Viking, 133–134
Vinland, xii
Vǫlsunga saga, 118, 155, 167
Volund, 155
Vǫlundarkviða, 155, 167

Wagner, Richard, xi, 3, 135
Wagner, Wilhelm, 135
Walpole, Horace, 38
Wawn, Andrew, xi
Werenskiold, Erik, 142
Whistler, Charles Watts, 138
Widsith, 26
Wilson, David M., 71, 94
Winged helmets, 110, 133, 138
Winnick, Katheryn, 4
Winroth, Anders, 77
Wolin, 16
Woodcarving, 44
World War I, xii
World War II, xii
Worm, Ole, 155–157
Wychwood Warriors, 123

York, ix, 16, 123–124, 149

About the Authors

Kirsten Wolf is the Kim Nilsson Professor and the Torger Thompson Chair of Scandinavian Studies in the Department of German, Nordic, and Slavic at the University of Wisconsin–Madison. She has published numerous books and articles on Old Norse-Icelandic language and literature and aspects of life and culture in Viking Age Scandinavia.

Tristan Mueller-Vollmer is a doctoral candidate in Scandinavian Studies in the Department of German, Nordic, and Slavic at the University of Wisconsin–Madison. His research focuses on Old Norse-Icelandic, runology, onomastics (the study of names), and the mythology, religion, and visual culture of pre-Christian Scandinavia. His dissertation explores personal names on Viking Age runestones.

www.ingramcontent.com/pod-product-compliance
Lightning Source LLC
Chambersburg PA
CBHW070300230426
43664CB00014B/2594